CRYST. AL
PALACE F.C.

1990-2011
MORE BIASED COMMENTARY

Written and illustrated by Chris Winter
With a foreword by Jo Brand

RED
POST
PRESS

First edition published in 2011 by

Red Post Press

© 2011 Chris Winter
ISBN 978-0-9516636-3-9

Also available :

"Crystal Palace F.C. 1969-1990:
A Biased Commentary"

ISBN 978-0-9516636-2-2

Contents

Dedicated
to
Len

Foreword by Jo Brand

Bit of a latecomer to league football, but I became a devoted and passionate supporter of Crystal Palace from the early 70s when I moved to London and lived in Thornton Heath.

Selhurst Park is a great venue, shoehorned into the back end of South East London and I love the fans who are good, down to earth sort of people - if you apply the Roy Keane "prawn sandwich" criteria! I love the atmosphere, the Long Good Friday theme when the Eagles come through the tunnel and the roar of anticipation from the supporters.

The Palace are a proper 'local' team - sometimes shockingly bad and others just sublime. Inconsistencies in performance keep you agonising over league tables, then somehow, against all the odds they bounce back and once again you're on that roller coaster of hope, anxiety and euphoria.

I don't get to matches all that often but find myself faintly preoccupied on a Saturday afternoon, awaiting the outcome. It's great feeling part of the Club and I look forward to a time when I can regularly totter to a seat in the stands for a full 90 minutes of Crystal Palace football.

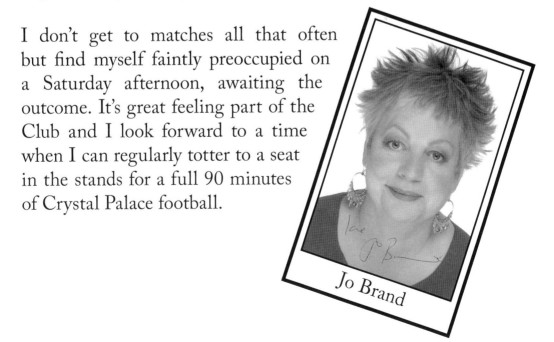

Jo Brand

Introduction

This volume follows on from "A Biased Commentary" which covered my first 21 years of supporting Palace between 1969 and 1990. It has taken me another 21 years to finally get around to updating this very personal history, but I hope that you find plenty in the words and pictures to bring back some fond memories of your own. For much of my time as a Palace fan I have had the privilege of providing live match day commentaries from the back of the Arthur Wait stand to patients in Mayday Hospital, and to blind and partially-sighted fans at the ground, and there is no shame in admitting that my description of the action has always been utterly biased, hence the title and the tone of this book.

They say that it's never boring supporting Palace, but even if that's not always exactly true there is always the certainty that something unexpected and often bizarre is just around the corner. The period since 1990 has seen some extraordinary swings in Palace's fortunes; a series of unlikely promotions, twice on the verge of extinction, occasional flirtation with relegation to the third tier, and countless highs and lows along the way. My aim with this book is to record my personal memories of some of the events and personalities that have made supporting Palace such a fascinating experience along with some of my opinions, both considered and prejudiced. I have tried not to include too many statistics; I would recommend Ian King's excellent book "Crystal Palace: The Complete Record" to anyone looking for the facts and figures.

I have chosen my fantasy team from everyone who has played for Palace during that time and I give my thoughts on my favourite players in each position in the final chapters, but for the sake of a good argument my team is as follows:

Nigel Martyn

John Humphrey   Eric Young   Fan Zhiyi   Dean Gordon

David Hopkin   Aki Riihilahti

Attilio Lombardo   John Salako

Dougie Freedman   Andy Johnson

Thanks are due to Roger Dickson, Michael De Luca and Don Madgwick for their invaluable help with the production of this volume; to Dave Keeley and Richard Avison for their support and encouragement; to Jo Brand and Jayne Love for providing a wonderful foreword; to all the players who have given me so much enjoyment for so many years; and to Carol and Bud for their immense patience and a great deal more besides.

The story begins with Palace about to embark in their second season in what was then Division One under manager Steve Coppell. The partnership of Ian Wright and Mark Bright had been central to Palace's success, but Palace were yet to be taken seriously, despite recovering from a humiliating 9-0 defeat at Anfield to famously beat Liverpool 4-3 in the FA Cup semi-final. The 1989-90 season had ended with Palace's first ever FA Cup final, drawing a thrilling game 3-3 with Manchester United before losing 1-0 in a replay which wasn't quite so captivating.

1990-91

"When Geoff goes up to lift the Zenith Cup, we'll be there, we'll be there..."

The disappointment of missing out on the FA Cup might have been devastating, but Steve Coppell was fortunate that Palace's achievements back in the First Division still hadn't been fully acknowledged, and that their progress in the Cup was seen by many as just a tale of plucky underdogs. Consequently, he was able to keep hold of talent such as Wright, Bright, Thomas and Gray, since not too many believed them capable of developing into players worthy of playing at the highest level. He also made two superb signings in Eric Young, now reunited with Andy Thorn from the days of Wimbledon's Crazy Gang,

ANDY THORN

and Charlton's captain, right back John Humphrey. Another former Don, winger Glyn Hodges, was also signed during the summer, but it was the two new defenders who made all the difference in what was to turn out to be Palace's best ever season. The defensive unit of Nigel Martyn, Humphrey, Thorn, Young and Richard Shaw was rarely disrupted throughout the whole season, and this gave Palace the sort of stability that Terry Venables had created a decade earlier with Burridge, Hinshelwood, Sansom, Cannon and Gilbert.

Young scored on his debut on Luton's plastic pitch, and although an away draw seemed a pretty humdrum start to the season, the next game was a cracking 2-1 defeat of Chelsea, Andy Gray scoring an early penalty then getting sent off with Dennis Wise, and Ian Wright floating a peach of a winner over Dave Beasant. That game on a hot August night attracted a decent crowd of over 27,000, and was the first time that the front of the Arthur Wait stand was all seated, but home attendances continued to be generally poor, a fact bemoaned by Steve Coppell later in the season. As autumn edged in, Palace went ten games without defeat, and it wasn't until they met Manchester United at the beginning of November that they lost in the league, by which time they were sitting fourth in the table. The high point, though, was a 3-0 victory at Norwich which saw Palace end the day in second position, after putting on a thoroughly convincing display of fluid, attacking football with John Salako really looking the part, and despite missing the injured Mark Bright.

The impetus continued in the League Cup, when Wright and Bright both scored hat-tricks during an 8-0 pasting of Southend, and after such a fine start to the season, there was a gradually dawning realisation the Palace had some genuinely good players. Eric Young and Glyn Hodges were already part of the Wales setup, but England were starting to show interest in Nigel Martyn, Ian Wright and - controversially for some - Geoff Thomas, and the trio were chosen for the England B squad by new manager Graham Taylor. Although Taylor hadn't yet been cast as a complete incompetent by the press, he had been stuck with the "route one" label from his days at Watford, and although he had since won promotion and then second place in the league with Aston Villa, this counted for nothing to some of the lazier and more supercilious of the press corps. Otherwise decent football writers such as David Lacey chose to pour similar scorn on Coppell's Palace, deriding the long ball as an affront to cultured souls such as he, the guardian of some pure and mythical version of the game. Throughout the season, it seemed that nobody could accept that Palace were the third best team that year, behind Arsenal and Liverpool, yet when they beat Liverpool 1-0 at the end of December, it was an accurate marker of just how far Palace had progressed since that 9-0 hammering just over a year earlier. Coppell was the first to admit that their game was robust, even simple, but it required a high level of discipline throughout the team, and this was the year that it all came together and gave the fans a team to be really proud of. If winning the ball and getting it quickly forward to strikers of the calibre of Bright and Wright proved irksome to some, it marked out Steve Coppell as a most astute manager, although he had to grow a pretty thick skin at the time.

Coppell read the riot act to his players after they scraped past Orient and then lost to Southampton in the League Cup, despite playing a full strength side - this was the days before the League Cup was seen as an irritant - but Palace continued to make quiet progress in the Full Members (Zenith Data Systems) Cup, which was eventually to lead them to Wembley once again. Winter set in with a vengeance during January, and the dream of returning to claim the FA Cup was over before it had begun after an epic third round tie against Nottingham Forest. A goalless draw at Selhurst Park forced a replay at the City Ground, but torrential rain meant a wasted journey for fans and players alike, as the game was called off only an hour before kick-off. The tie eventually took place the following week,

in thickening fog, and was notable for John Salako's equaliser in the final minute, to force another replay. A misplaced back pass by Forest's youngster Roy Keane led to Crossley's wayward clearance falling to Salako, who lifted it delightfully over the keeper from fully 40 yards; according to Keane, he returned to the dressing room and a fist in the face from Brian Clough. A week later, another trip to Nottingham for the second replay ended with the home side winning 3-0, and then a few days later the teams met once again in the league, again at The City Ground, and this time Eric Young popped up with a headed goal to win the game for Palace.

This consolidated Palace's position in the table, third behind Liverpool and Arsenal, and with a little gap opening up to Leeds and Manchester United. Although the league form became patchy from then on, and despite losing 4-0 at Highbury and 3-0 at Anfield, Palace were well enough placed to start thinking realistically about the prospect of a place in Europe the following season, which third place might ensure. More pressing, though, was the matter of the ZDS Cup, known to many as the Mickey Mouse Cup. Part of the reason that the competition was treated as such a joke was that it was dreamt up by the universally loathed Chelsea chairman Ken Bates and our own Ron Noades in the wake of the European ban on English clubs, following the Heysel atrocity in 1985, although the biggest clubs didn't bother to enter in any case. Nevertheless, it was designed to bring in some gate money and offer a chance of winning some sort of trophy to perpetual under-achievers such as Chelsea, Manchester City and Everton, without them having the inconvenience of getting past the likes of Liverpool and Arsenal.

The route to the final was mundane, victories against Bristol Rovers, Brighton and Luton leading to a two-legged semi-final against Norwich notable for the first start in the team for the promising Gareth Southgate. Although the crowds thus far had been quite meagre, the atmosphere at Wembley, with over 50,000 turning out for the final against Everton, was extraordinary, lacking the overwhelming tension and trepidation of a year earlier. Was I the only one who thought it was one of the club's greatest days, and were the rest of you singing just to humour me? On that day it felt like we were one of the best teams in the country,

GEOFF THOMAS

and beating Everton so soundly seemed to confirm that view, although it remained a closely guarded secret throughout the rest of the country. It was a glorious distillation of the style of play that had brought Palace such success all season, with Geoff Thomas showing all his leadership qualities in midfield and scoring the first with a diving header, the defence holding firm throughout, and Ian Wright nicking two goals in typical fashion. Even John Salako bagged himself a rare header. Again, Palace were accused of being too physical, and indeed Everton's Martin Keown took it upon himself to exact revenge on Eric Young in a league game two weeks later, for which he was rightly sent off. However

the game was seen by neutrals, it was a great feeling as a Palace fan to see my team dominate a hard fought Cup Final, and shout my heart out when Geoff Thomas lifted a trophy at Wembley. Give me that; I may never experience it again.

Here we were then, in the spring of 1991, among the top sides in England, with Ian Wright having represented his country on a freezing Wembley night against Cameroon, with Thomas and Martyn pressing for places in the full squad, and with our European place almost assured. Steve Coppell had built a side to challenge the best, and the only way was up. Arsenal had sealed the title already, and Liverpool were sitting second in the table, despite Kenny Dalglish inexplicably resigning as manager, but the second European spot was ours. Liverpool had been held responsible for the Heysel atrocity which led to an indefinite European ban on English clubs, and a further three year ban on top for Liverpool themselves; with UEFA having voted to allow English clubs back into competitions in 1990, Liverpool were due to spend another two years in the wilderness. Unaccountably, disgracefully, the FA then colluded with UEFA to overturn the original decision, and allow Liverpool back two years early, so destroying Palace's first ever opportunity to compete in Europe. Many other teams had been denied a European place since 1985, but to have that prize snatched away so late in the day was an absolute outrage, and proved catastrophic for the club and the fans. As director Geoff Geraghty wrote in the final programme of the season: "The whole thing stinks! I can't think of another body of incompetent, senile, decrepit old fogeys who sit in judgement on our national game anywhere in the world."

1991-92

"I'm not being racist, but..."

The question is not whether Ron Noades is a racist - those close to him have testified emphatically in his defence, and his wife Novello publicly sported a t-shirt proclaiming that "my husband is not a racist" - but whether his words could be construed as such. Let's see: "One of the problems with black players is I don't think too many can read the game... You get an awful lot with great pace, great athletes, love to play with the ball in front of them, but when it's behind, it's chaos... The black players at this club lend the side a lot of skill and flair, but you also need white players in there to balance things up and give the team some brains and some common sense." Oh, dear.

Ron Noades is nothing if not blunt, so it should have been obvious that for him to take part in a TV programme about black footballers becoming managers, and to allow himself to be filmed speaking his mind was going to be a huge mistake. Noades protested that he was stitched up by Channel 4 and Garth Crooks, the presenter of the programme "Great Britain Limited", and that his comments were all taken out of context, but I must say that as I watched the show I was cringing with embarrassment. Palace's recent success owed a massive amount to black players; not just Wright and Bright, but Andy Gray, Eric Young, John Salako, and Richard Shaw were first team regulars, and perhaps that was why I was so shocked to hear these absurd statements from Noades. It could have gone no further than us shaking our heads and just praying that he would shut up, but the press made a meal of it and reported that Noades' comments had caused turmoil among the players. Whatever the truth, it felt at the time as though this must have played a part in Ian Wright's departure to

Arsenal only weeks later, although from this distance I suspect that his decision to leave Palace had more to do with us having been robbed of our rightful place in Europe.

IAN WRIGHT

The season started well enough, with a couple of new faces, but with the core of the successful team of the previous year intact. Wright and Bright were still together up front, Thomas and Gray in midfield, Salako and McGoldrick on the wings, and new signing Lee Sinnott filling in for Eric Young alongside Andy Thorn, as Young had still not recovered from Martin Keown's assault the previous April. Coppell started to fiddle with the defence, sometimes using McGoldrick as a sweeper in a five-man back line, and utilising Sinnott in a variety of positions, none of which he particularly shone in. After a defeat at Manchester City in their first game, Palace won three on the trot and things were looking good until a heavy defeat at home to Arsenal shortly after Noades' ill-advised outpourings. Injuries to Richard Shaw and Geoff Thomas were disruptive enough, but the news that Ian Wright was heading to Highbury came out of the blue, and seemed to surprise Coppell as much as anyone. He was moved to write a letter to fans explaining that "Ian had been unsettled for some time and I had tried very hard to put my finger on exactly what was wrong. It did become obvious to me that Ian wanted to move to further his career and he expressed the desire to go to only one club which was Arsenal. Ian had a clause in his contract that stated 'should a club come in for him who could offer him European football he would be free to leave us for that club...' Had we turned the bid down, we would have had a situation where a player was not happy with us and would not have given us 100% effort and commitment."

The £2.5million fee seemed at the time an absolute steal, but what really hurt was that Wright's desire to move confirmed that, however great the strides Palace had made over the past couple of years, we were destined never to be seen as a truly big club, and that was the moment that the rot set in. From Wright's point of view, he did absolutely the right thing, and went on to be top scorer that season in Division One, top scorer for Arsenal for six successive seasons, and break Cliff Bastin's club goal scoring record. It remains a mystery to me why Wright never really clicked for England, and why Graham Taylor chose to take Alan Smith and Nigel Clough to Sweden for Euro 92, but leave Ian and Geoff Thomas at home. I feel privileged to have followed Ian Wright from his first appearance as a substitute against Huddersfield in 1985, through his alchemical partnership with Mark Bright, and countless wonderful goals including in the Division Two play-off final, the FA Cup final and the ZDS final - yes, I still cling on to that as a great memory. I was never lucky enough to see Johnny Byrne play, but he is the only player in Palace's entire history to be mentioned in the same breath as Wright, and I doubt that I will ever see a finer footballer at Selhurst Park, but who knows when another rough diamond might turn up out of nowhere.

If anyone thought that Mark Bright would flounder without his erstwhile partner he proved them wrong, proceeding to score in eight consecutive games and complete the season as the only ever-present player, but Coppell had an immediate problem of how to fill Ian Wright's boots up front. John Salako had been used to good effect as a striker on occasions, as well as in goal after Nigel Martyn was sent off against Wimbledon, and was in the form of his life. After a splendid performance on the wing for England against Germany, he was looking assured of a good many caps for his country, and it was a massive blow when he was badly injured in a game against Leeds in October, after he fell awkwardly and a defender landed on his left knee. As expected, Salako was out for the rest of the season, and coming so soon after Wright's exit, this was a massive setback for Coppell. Rather than take a chance on giving young Stan Collymore a run in the side, as he was more than a little green, the manager splashed out a reported £1.8 million for

MARCO GABBIADINI

Marco Gabbiadini from Sunderland, a player who had scored freely for the Black Cats in the Third and Second Divisions, but who had so far flopped in Division One. As paltry as the fee for Wright had appeared, the sum paid for Gabbiadini seemed ridiculously inflated, but most of

Steve Coppell's signings to date had turned out to be well judged, so there was a feeling of optimism among fans that he might have landed a bit of a coup. At the time it was rumoured that Palace had been looking at a few strikers, including Southampton's burgeoning Alan Shearer, and even now it's painful to think what might have been. Not only was Gabbiadini not a patch on Ian Wright, he wasn't a patch on the Gabbiadini that had hit the headlines a couple of seasons earlier, and Steve Coppell later admitted that he had signed him based on his past reputation, and hadn't seen him play. The high point of his Palace career was hitting the winner in a 2-1 victory over Liverpool at Anfield, but despite the odd goal he never looked at home in a Palace shirt, and was offloaded only four months later to Derby, at a huge loss. There was talk in the press of bust-ups in the dressing room, and certainly Andy Gray left soon afterwards, but it was hard to disagree with the damning verdict of Assistant Manager Alan Smith that Gabbiadini was "incredibly average".

Gray himself had managed half a game in an England shirt, and increasingly gave the impression that he felt he had outgrown Selhurst Park, which didn't endear him to the fans or the manager. Coppell commented that "it is a bit tiresome when you come in every morning and there is one person who really is a cloud over everyone else's training", and made it clear that his time was up. Gray's move to Spurs marked the start of his decline from the top level, and it was hard not to smile to oneself when hearing that his next port of call was Marbella. Another player to fall foul of Coppell was Paul Bodin, who by rights should have benefited from Richard Shaw's absence through injury for most of the season, but the manager preferred the unremarkable Lee Sinnott at left back, and

eventually sold Bodin back to Swindon at a loss, remarking that "he is basically a failed First Division footballer - if he is a good player he will prove his point with Swindon and throw the ball back in my face in a few years' time", which seemed uncharacteristically unkind.

PAUL BODIN

John Salako's injury gave Simon Rodger the chance to make his debut, but he in turn was injured, so Coppell leafed through the Rothman's Yearbook looking for left-footed players, and came up with the name of Paul Mortimer, who had only been at Aston Villa for a few months, having signed from Charlton. He took up the offer of an early return to London, but Mortimer was also blighted by injuries so Rodger eventually settled into the side, making a name for himself as a hard working, energetic and reliable player, who I always thought of as somewhere between Geoff Thomas and Phil Barber. Gareth Southgate also started to cement his place in the side, and there were occasional starts for other youth team graduates Simon Osborn, David Whyte, Dean Gordon and Jamie Moralee. For the last couple of months of the season, Mark Bright's partner up front was Chris Coleman, a young Welshman bought from Swansea as a full back, who did a decent job of putting himself about

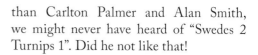

and causing defenders a few problems in the air. There were a few good results to come, notably a 1-0 defeat of Liverpool, completing the double, and prompting the ever sensitive Graeme Souness to whinge "I feel as if I've been mugged."

DAVID WHYTE

As the season wore on, Palace slowly slipped from a high point of fifth in the table to end up very comfortably in tenth place, and it seems strange now to remember that this was a disappointment after doing so well the year before, because, after all, it still represents the second best season in Palace's history. More than the loss of Wright and Gray, more than the succession of bad transfer deals, what troubled me most as a Palace fan that season was the constant sniping from sections of the media, who continued to denigrate Palace as "bully boys", which must have started to erode the players' confidence, and which was typified by the general reaction to Geoff Thomas' inclusion in the England team. Even now, he is remembered more for a single wayward shot against France than for the fact that England were unbeaten in the nine games that he played, and that is simply down to the view that he played for an inferior club, who had no right rubbing shoulders with the elite. If Graham Taylor had taken Geoff Thomas and Ian Wright to Sweden for that summer's European Championship, rather than Carlton Palmer and Alan Smith, we might never have heard of "Swedes 2 Turnips 1". Did he not like that!

1992-93

"This penalty can give Palace three vital points. Why is Southgate taking it?"

Maybe Coppell himself had by now got a little bored with Palace's customary direct style, and certainly the public seemed to be turned off, with attendances slipping and fans voicing regular criticism of the manager. He spoke before the season started of the need for more subtlety, and of how predictable they had become. Perhaps he had already decided to ring the changes, but the talk was of John Salako returning from ten months out injured to be Mark Bright's new strike partner. As it turned out, Salako was introduced on the wing to ease his way back in, and Coppell persisted with Chris Coleman for a few games,

CHRIS COLEMAN

starting a sequence of four draws with the season's opener against Blackburn. Kenny Dalglish's team had invested big money, including bringing in 22-year-old Alan Shearer, and we were immediately reminded of what we had missed out on when he scored two top class goals, although our own Gareth Southgate scored a long-range corker himself from midfield.

Palace's own early transfer dealings were decidedly underwhelming, non-league players Stuart Massey and Martyn O'Connor arriving along with Wigan

defender Darren Patterson, and Rudi Hedman and Perry Suckling moving on. Eddie McGoldrick had been holding out for a move, but eventually signed a new contract, and speculation about Geoff Thomas going to either Arsenal or Blackburn came to nothing, although it did appear to noticeably unsettle the skipper. Having spoken about the need for a new partner for Bright, someone who could score double figures, September saw the arrival of a striker who turned out to be Coppell's best signing for several years. Chris Armstrong arrived from Millwall for a million pound fee, but only started twice alongside Mark Bright before Bright himself was sold out of the blue to Sheffield Wednesday. Bright later described how he knew nothing about Wednesday's interest until Coppell told him: "Trevor Francis has tried to buy you two or three times, I think the time might be right for you to move." There were rumblings that Steve Coppell was trying to modify Palace's game, and move away from the long ball, and the player who came from Wednesday as part of the deal was Paul Williams, a very different type of forward to Bright.

PAUL WILLIAMS

It wasn't until late September that Palace recorded a victory, Armstrong scoring twice away to Everton, and the first home win didn't come until early December, against

Sheffield United. Luck seemed to have deserted Palace, and there were so many games where they threw away a lead, and ended up drawing games which they could have won, memorably the game at Ipswich when Gareth Southgate smacked a penalty against the post in the last minute. Four years later I watched horrified as Gareth grabbed the ball in the Euro '96 semi-final and stepped up to take that crucial penalty...

GARETH SOUTHGATE

The one bright spot was John Salako's return to form, and as well as hitting a wonderful goal to put Southampton out of the League Cup, he was recalled for the England squad to face Norway in a World Cup qualifier. He made the bench for that game, but that was to be his last appearance at Wembley, as bad luck struck again, and he was forced to return to the States for further surgery, which meant him missing another season, and led some to doubt whether he would ever recover.

November ended badly, with a 5-0 humiliation at Anfield, and there wasn't much to be optimistic about when Palace returned three days later to face Liverpool again in the League Cup. Chris Armstrong was cup-tied, Paul Williams - yet to score a goal - was injured, and Coppell decided to start with the untried Bobby Bowry and George Ndah, with Grant Watts on the bench. McGoldrick reverted to sweeper and Coleman returned up front, heading the goal that meant a replay at Selhurst Park, and prompting yet another petulant whine from Graeme Souness, despite Liverpool equalising through the softest of penalties. As the Evening Standard put it: "Souness' ill-timed, ill-tempered and ill-informed outburst was perhaps just a smokescreen to cover Liverpool's shortcomings." Suddenly, Palace's season came to life, and December saw a run of five straight league wins which lifted them from the doldrums to fifteenth in the table, and there was that thrilling League Cup replay against Liverpool. Again, Bowry started in midfield with Osborn, and Grant Watts marked his first start with a headed goal to put Palace ahead before Liverpool drew level with another penalty. Shocking defending by Steve Nicol let in Andy Thorn to head the winner, and Palace progressed to face Chelsea in the quarter-final. Steve Coppell even won a Manager of the Month award, unimaginable just a few weeks earlier.

With Lee Sinnott and Paul Mortimer being placed on the transfer list, and Collymore shipped out to Southend, the squad was looking rather stretched, but again the youngsters played their part in defeating Chelsea, to send Palace into the League Cup semi-final. On a filthy January night, both Grant Watts and George Ndah scored in the 3-1 victory, but it was Chris Coleman's goal which lingers in the memory. The pitch was a quagmire around both penalty areas, and when Frank Sinclair poked a back pass towards Kevin Hitchcock in goal, Coleman was alert enough to spot that the ball had ground to a halt in the mud, and pounced on it before the stranded keeper. Even as he wheeled away in celebration, the ball seemed to take an age to dribble into the goal, before coming to rest exhausted just over the line.

That single moment turned out to be the high point of the season, as Palace continued to struggle with injuries to Thomas, Southgate and Williams, and failed to get in any new players of note. Despite Armstrong shining, and scoring fifteen times, goals continued to prove hard to come by, and the ever-present Eddie McGoldrick was second-highest league scorer with eight, pretty good for someone playing almost every position except as a striker. Arsenal beat Palace in both legs of the League Cup semi-final, Hartlepool dumped Palace out of the FA Cup, and the season trudged towards its conclusion with the familiar story of tight games ending in draws, each dropped point seeing Palace slide closer to the danger area and relegation.

goalless draw at Manchester City meant that Palace went into the final game at Arsenal three points clear of relegation, and with better goal difference than Oldham, with Middlesbrough and Forest already down. Surely Ian Wright wouldn't score against us, surely Arsenal wouldn't win 3-0, surely Oldham wouldn't win 4-3 at Southampton! Of course they did, and what a miserable anti-climax it was to what had been a pretty glum season all round. It didn't take Steve Coppell too long to decide that he'd had enough, and after almost nine years at the club, he swiftly and quietly resigned.

GEORGE NDAH

With three games to go, captain Geoff Thomas wrote in the programme that "Our fate is in our own hands and, assuming we get four points from our remaining three games, we shall remain in the Premier League even if our rivals win all their outstanding matches". Sadly, Geoff had his sums wrong. The players did a lap of honour after beating Ipswich, and then a

"That's Armstrong's first hat-trick for Palace, and it won't be his last!"

With Steve Coppell gone, the time seemed right for Geoff Thomas to move on, to Wolves, and who could blame Eddie McGoldrick for jumping at the chance to join Ian Wright at Arsenal? Thomas had suffered a frustrating season all round, unsettled by transfer talk, disrupted by injury and loss of form, and we were all ready for a bit of a change. It would have been no surprise to see the likes of Young, Thorn, and especially Nigel Martyn leave the club, especially since Martyn seemed in pole position to become England's regular keeper. It was great news that all three chose to stay, along with John Humphrey, and with Salako due to return once again from his long rehabilitation and Chris Armstrong already having shown real quality, there was at least good reason to be more optimistic about the coming season. That was tempered somewhat by the fact that no new players arrived during the summer, so there was a nagging feeling that the emerging younger players such as Southgate, Rodger, Osborne and Bowry would be carrying the weight of too much expectation.

Of perhaps more concern was that chairman Ron Noades had decided not to look elsewhere for a new manager, but gave Coppell's assistant Alan Smith his chance. Smith had been at the club since 1982 with responsibility for youth development, which had seen the emergence of John Salako and Richard Shaw, and had looked after the reserves before ending up as Steve Coppell's right hand man. Given the revisionism that swiftly followed Coppell's resignation, the appointment of Smith could have smacked of "same shit, different shovel", but before the season began both Noades and Smith went to great lengths to assure the fans that they would be playing a new style, which Smith liked to call "pass and move".

We'd heard much the previous season about Palace trying to change their style, but the criticism of Coppell was that he was by inclination too negative, and was too ready to revert to Palace's customary long ball approach when things weren't going well. I never saw it that way, and always felt that he was simply being pragmatic. He adapted his team according to what he thought was needed at any given point in a game, and was desperately unfortunate that it didn't pay off at the very end of what had been a really difficult season on and off the pitch. Ron Noades never came across as a "hands-off" proprietor, and expressed his views in some detail: "I personally did not enjoy the last two seasons... I felt that we were

CHRIS ARMSTRONG

getting more and more introspective and more fearful of the opposition as each week went by... I don't want to see our best attacking players used at home to defend against the other team's full backs and I don't want to see us playing sweeper systems at home against the likes of Everton and Coventry when I think we should be attacking them and winning matches." Smith was also explicit in outlining his vision to the fans: "I ask you for your continued support and encouragement to play the open, flowing football that I believe will earn us promotion. I, Steve Harrison and David Kemp have introduced a style of play you will enjoy." Fine words butter no parsnips, thought the sceptics among us, but we were wrong, and very happy to be so wrong.

Things didn't start too well, with only a point and no goals from the first two games, but Smith stuck to his guns and suddenly everything just fell into place. Nottingham Forest came to Selhurst parading their new £2.2million signing Stan Collymore, who had sloped off to Southend from Palace less than a year previously, but with Paul Williams looking much happier alongside Armstrong, and Southgate working well with Shaw in midfield, Palace embarked on a glorious run of six wins and two draws, playing throughout with real panache. The mood was typified by the home game against Portsmouth, which ranks as one my favourites of all time, not just because of the 5-1 scoreline, but because the team were playing with exactly the kind of open flowing style we had been promised.

Chris Armstrong's luscious hat-trick wasn't even the highlight, that honour going to Gareth Southgate's stunning solo goal, one which for me brought back memories of John "Yogi Bear" Hughes against Sheffield United many years ago. Southgate had started out at Palace as a defender, playing at right back and centre back, but during this vintage season he came into his own as a midfielder of rare quality. He got in a tackle wide on the left, deep inside his own half, dinked it past the challenger, then strode unchecked over the half way line into a great chasm where the Pompey midfield should have been. He might have thought about laying it off, but went for goal himself and without breaking stride lashed the ball past the keeper from well outside the area. That goal was the making of him as he grew in confidence to become a key player in the Number 4 shirt, taking over the captain's armband with distinction

after Andy Thorn's injury in November and scoring a host of similarly swashbuckling goals throughout the season.

Williams had a spell up front, clearly relishing Palace's new brand of passing football, and David Whyte showed glimpses of real flair, which meant Chris Coleman settling into his proper defensive role, but without doubt the star turn was Chris Armstrong. His gait looked a little awkward, but with the ball at his feet he had an instinctive ability to outpace the last man and get his shot on target from any distance. He was terrific in the air as well, getting on the end of Rodger and Salako's crosses rather than having to fight for the ball hoofed from the back; I was moved to sport a t-shirt with a picture of Armstrong celebrating, and the caption "Ian who?"

RICKY NEWMAN

With Dean Gordon coming in at left back, Coleman switching to the centre alongside Young, and Humphrey and Shaw fighting it out for the right back spot, the defensive unit became tighter as the season progressed, and by Christmas Palace were top of the division, where they were to stay for the rest of the season. John Salako marked his long-awaited return from injury with a hat-trick against Stoke, and Simon Rodger was establishing himself down the left, but

cracks were starting to appear, and there were still a couple of perceived weaknesses which Alan Smith needed to address to make sure the team didn't slip up in their quest to get back into the Premier League. In midfield, the youngsters Osborne, Bowry and Ricky Newman all succumbed to injury at various points, and Smith filled the gap very effectively with Damien Matthew from Chelsea who did a good job down the right and looked a cut above, particularly in terms of physical presence. The real coup, though, was the loan signing of Paul Stewart, the

DAMIEN MATTHEW

former Spurs and England striker who had fallen out with Graeme Souness - a recommendation in itself - and slipped down the pecking order at Liverpool behind Ian Rush, Robbie Fowler and Nigel Clough (yes, really). Stewart immediately added that bit of aggression and power that neither the nimble Williams nor Whyte could offer, and although not prolific, he got through an awful lot of work up front, on and off the ball, which allowed Armstrong to continue to flourish.

This was a good season for "concentrating on the league", and before going out of the League Cup to Everton after a replay, and to Wolves in the FA Cup, there was the small matter of the newly reconstituted Anglo-Italian Cup (now that the Full Members'

Cup had died a death, mourned by few). I had been there at Selhurst Park in 1971 to see Luigi Riva play for Cagliari, and Bobby Tambling score the winner for Palace. I didn't make it to the San Siro to see Tambling's two goals sink Inter Milan, but this time, at last, I was determined that I would make it to a game in Europe. The furthest we got was Woolwich, where Palace lost to Charlton before beating Millwall at home, and Europe would have to wait. I've heard that Brescia isn't up to much in any case.

Another great success in this Championship season was local boy Dean Gordon, possibly the most one-footed player I've ever watched, but by Jiminy, what a left foot! He thumped home a couple of unstoppable penalties, but most memorably cannoned in a spectacular late equaliser against Derby to help Palace to their second nine-game unbeaten run of the season. From that moment, every time he advanced down the left to within range, we would expect another belter, and he'd generally pop up with one or two for each of the next four seasons. Gordon, Coleman, Southgate, Rodger and Armstrong all grew up very quickly that year, and Palace coasted to the title with a run of six straight wins putting them seven points clear of runners-up Forest before an anti-climactic home defeat to Watford, but the jubilant celebrations reflected a season in the starkest possible contrast to a year earlier, one which - as Alan Smith had pledged - was ultimately a sheer joy to witness.

1994-95

"I think that maybe it's like a dream for some people sometimes, to kick these kinds of people. So I did it for them. So they are happy."

That was Eric Cantona in 2011, still talking total tosh sixteen years after the event.

There had been plenty going on under the surface as Palace won promotion the previous season, but as long as results had been going well, not too much was made of it. Alan Smith had seen fit to have a purge of his unwieldy squad, though why John Humphrey was sent on loan for a while to Reading remained a mystery. Among the players not making the cut for the new campaign were Paul Mortimer and Lee Sinnott, and in a characteristically poor bit of business for Palace, Charlton took David Whyte and some cash in return for Darren Pitcher. What was blindingly obvious was that we needed a new striker, not a new right back, nor a superannuated Ray "Butch" Wilkins ambling around the midfield. Perhaps he could have done a job for Palace, who he had been so dismissive of as a TV pundit covering the FA Cup Final in 1990, but we never found out since he broke his foot in the very first game and never played for Palace again. Alan Smith had wanted to keep Paul Stewart, but couldn't agree terms with Liverpool, so was left with the same problem that he had identified before Stewart arrived, that of finding a worthy partner for Chris Armstrong. It was certain to be much tougher for Armstrong in the Premier League, and if money was to be spent to keep Palace up, the priority had to be a strong target man. Everyone said so, and everyone kept saying so after the new man was revealed: not the Swedish World Cup star Kennet Anderson, whose signature was supposedly in the bag, but Armstrong's best mate from Wrexham, latterly making a few waves at Stockport, Andy Preece. By all accounts Preece was on holiday with Armstrong when he got the call, and the word was that he'd been signed as a sop to Armstrong, who was being courted for big money by Everton. That lack of real investment at the start of such a crucial season, whatever the reasoning, will always be cited as Noades' biggest error, and that is not just with the benefit of hindsight. I'm sure that it wasn't just every single fan who thought that, but Alan Smith as well.

BRUCE DYER

Bruce Dyer, a teenage prodigy from Watford, had signed towards the end of the promotion season for over a million pounds, but was still very raw, so Preece lined up alongside Armstrong, with Pitcher and Wilkins replacing Humphrey and Matthew respectively for the first game, at home to Liverpool. What an unmitigated disaster, Pitcher making an impression only by giving the ball away for Liverpool's third of six goals, Preece taken to hospital with a back injury, and Wilkins leaving the ground that afternoon on crutches. Looking for some crumb of comfort, at least Chris Armstrong scored Palace's solitary goal, but it was to be his last in the league until November, some thirteen games later. We were in for a very long, hard season, but this turned out to be perhaps the least predictable year I can recall. The next six games resulted in four draws, with the defence paradoxically improving with the inclusion of Darren Patterson, but nevertheless there was very little expectation that the season's first victory would come at Highbury, of all places. Naturally, Ian Wright scored for the Gunners, but John Salako's brace secured a famous, and rare, triumph over Arsenal, to the massive delight of the brave souls who had dared to return to North London after that miserable relegation day two years earlier. Two more narrow defeats followed, but then a run of four straight wins left Palace in 10th place, a massive achievement following that first day debacle.

ANDY PREECE

Yet still goals were at a premium, and as Palace went on an unprecedented run of nine league games without scoring, it was clear that Armstrong was becoming a shadow of the player he had been. Salako, Preece and Dyer all had spells up front, and none of them provided the answer, but there was at least some good news in the League Cup, an impressive 4-1 defeat of Villa setting up a quarter final against Manchester City, which saw a rare start for the almost forgotten George Ndah, as City were dispatched 4-0.

That City game was one of the two home games I missed that season, as I was working evenings for a while, and the other

one came just a fortnight later against Manchester United, but at least I was able to listen to full commentary on the radio as United were welcomed to South London. It turned out to be one of the most infamous nights in Selhurst Park's history, and although I would normally have been way over the other side of the ground, in my commentary box in the back corner of the Arthur Wait stand, I still feel that I missed out somehow. I must even confess that in the aftermath, whenever I discussed the Cantona "Kung Fu" incident with neutrals, I would never actually say that I had witnessed it first hand, but equally would never volunteer the fact that I hadn't. United were pressing Blackburn for the title and the undisputed star of the show was "King Eric" Cantona. He had been voted PFA Player of the Year as United won the title in 1994, but was as arrogant as he was talented, a short fuse helping him collect a fair few red cards already.

Strutting around as usual, posing with his artfully upturned collar, he took exception to the fact that Richard Shaw had the temerity to man-mark him out of the game, and as a long clearance sailed over his head he aimed a petulant and spiteful kick at the Palace defender. The referee had no hesitation in showing the red card, and even Alex Ferguson in the away dugout appeared stoical, uncharacteristically unmoved to rant and rave at the decision. Cantona started to walk, paused, looked around as if to seek support from somewhere, and then accepting his fate with apparent dignity walked a little too theatrically along the touchline towards the exit. Naturally, the Palace fans closest to him were highly delighted, jeering as they would any opposition player sent off, but perhaps enjoying it even more given Cantona's notoriety, which he relished. Whatever insults were directed at the Frenchman, he suddenly reverted to type, and decided to pick a fight with someone in the crowd, attempting a leap over the advertising hoarding, and a flying kick to the fan's chest. He made some contact before falling in a clumsy heap and then picked himself up to land a blow with his fist before being dragged away down the tunnel. Listening on the radio, it sounded as if he had hurdled the barrier and gone into the crowd for a fight, but the pictures show that it was less dramatic than that, and more cowardly. Nevertheless, it was an outrageously childish reaction, and the ban that ensued would have been just as deserved had an anonymous lower league player committed the same criminal act of violence. A jail sentence was commuted to community service, on the grounds of provocation, viz: "they called me names."

The Manchester publicity machine, loyally supported by the more slavish sections of the media, tried to turn Cantona's thuggery into some kind of noble stance against racism, or swearing, or general abuse, but the FA, in a rare moment of wisdom, extended Cantona's ban to nine months. Cantona's famously enigmatic press conference shortly afterwards drew this priceless comment from his erstwhile team mate Gordon Strachan: "If a Frenchman goes on about seagulls, trawlers and sardines, he's called a philosopher. I'd just be called a short Scottish bum talking crap."

Cantona's recent reinvention of the incident as his personal crusade against hooliganism is pathetic, and unworthy of him. It is widely believed that United have some of the worst hooligans in the country following them and in the aftermath of the Cantona incident a group of Palace fans travelling to Villa Park for the FA Cup semi-final were reportedly ambushed, leading to the death of one of their number, Paul Nixon, from

multiple injuries. Cantona can't be held responsible, but perhaps he could consider not appearing quite so nauseatingly pleased with himself when recounting that infamous night.

The semi-final itself went to a replay after Palace had led twice and had chances to win it, and it was a measure of how far the shine had been taken off Palace's season that a disappointing replay, which United won 2-0, attracted fewer than 18,000 paying

DARREN PITCHER

customers. Despite the managers calling for calm in the aftermath of Nixon's death, Roy Keane was playing, so that was never going to happen. Palace's own would-be hard man Darren Pitcher made his mark on the Irishman with a tackle that left Keane needing stitches, and when Southgate made a fair tackle in the second half, Keane exacted delayed revenge with a vicious stamp on the prone Palace midfielder. This earned him his first red card in United colours, and provided a handy self-mythologising anecdote for his autobiography some years later.

Palace had also lost to Liverpool in the League Cup semi-final and were reeling from yet more controversy when it was revealed that Chris Armstrong had been suspended after testing positive for cannabis and "sent for counselling". This exposed the huge rift that had clearly developed between Alan Smith and Ron Noades, when Smith very pointedly called a press conference to neither confirm nor deny the real reason that Armstrong was missing from a Cup game against Watford, when Noades wanted the whole thing covered up, as is customary.

RAY HOUGHTON

Armstrong actually returned a sharper player, but his improvement was helped by the purchase in January of Iain Dowie, exactly the direct, powerful striker that we had needed all season. Like Paul Stewart before him, he didn't score too often, but led the line very effectively, and by April the experienced Ray Houghton had arrived from Aston Villa. Eight points from his first four games seemed to signal that Houghton was the man to save Palace's season, but there was a horrible inevitability about Palace losing five out of the last six games and being relegated once again. Last time it was on goal difference; this time they finished fourth from bottom, but for the first and last time four teams went down in order to reduce the Premier League to 20 teams. Founder members Palace may have been, but it was beginning to look like they weren't terribly welcome.

1995-96

"It's only a matter of time before the goals start flowing for Gareth Taylor."

Having parted company with Alan Smith, which in reality had been a long time coming, Ron Noades surprised everyone by bringing back Steve Coppell to the ill-defined role of "technical director". Given how disparaging the chairman had been about Coppell after relegation in 1993, this didn't bode too well, and I for one was curious as to why our most successful manager ever would want to work with Noades again, although responsibility for the first team was handed over to Ray Lewington, assisted by Palace old boy Peter Nicholas. After so many breathless and anxious seasons, a bit of mid-table mediocrity would have been welcome, and that was probably all we could hope for in any case, with so many players moving on during the summer. Gareth Southgate secured a well-deserved move to Aston Villa, where he went on to establish himself as a centre back, John Salako was off to Coventry, having fallen out of love with Selhurst Park, and Chris Armstrong went for £4.5 million to Spurs. Eric Young also left, for Wolves, but at least Chris Coleman, Richard Shaw, Iain Dowie and Nigel Martyn were there for the start of the season. By December though, Martyn was the only one still sticking around.

The new players to arrive were on the face of it uninspiring, but Marc Edworthy and David Hopkin slotted straight into the side for a storming 4-3 home win over Barnsley, during which Dowie scored his last two goals for Palace before moving to West Ham, with big Dutchman Jeroen Boere coming in part exchange. The other major signing, Millwall's Andy Roberts, was unfit until October, and with Boere also injured, again Palace had a shortage up front. Although Bruce Dyer was starting to show

his potential as a striker, two more forwards arrived soon after the start of the season: Barnet's 20-year-old Scot Dougie Freedman and the big money signing we had all been desperate for, Gareth Taylor from Bristol Rovers. Having started out as a centre-back, he had become a useful striker due to his height, and it seemed to take an eternity for Palace to finally land their man, the fee reported at the time as £1.25 million. Hopes were high that Palace had unearthed another young talent like Chris Armstrong, but it took Taylor twelve starts before he found the net, and by that time he had become the crowd's favourite scapegoat despite plenty of effort and a big dose of bad luck. He only scored one other goal, against Port Vale in the FA Cup, before being sold at a loss to Sheffield United, a bit of business reminiscent of the Gabbiadini fiasco.

MARC EDWORTHY

Freedman was a horse of a different colour though, and his quality was evident from the very start. The player he was most like in style was the underachieving Paul Williams, but he had the end result to go with the fancy footwork and clever positional sense. It was a great shame that Dowie had already left, for I am certain they would have formed a formidable partnership up front. The only other options for much of the season were Bruce Dyer, a revitalised

George Ndah back from a spell on loan at Bournemouth, and the 17-year-old Leon McKenzie, who scored on his debut in the League Cup, was voted man-of-the-match, and went home that night with his prize of a mountain bike.

With so many changes, and with Coleman and Shaw being sold to Blackburn and Coventry respectively as winter drew in, it was no surprise that Palace spent the first half of the season looking nervously down the table, despite some highly enjoyable successes; notably Dougie Freedman's first hat-trick against Eric Young's Wolves, and Dean Gordon's three goals away to West Brom, with two penalties and a rare header. David Hopkin had also impressed wide on the right or in central midfield, and Andy Roberts was starting to look a player of real quality after a delayed start to his Palace career. However, the pattern was of far too many draws, and an inability to get points from what should have been very winnable home games. A case in point was the home fixture against Millwall, when Bobby Bowry, who had moved to the Den along with Ricky Newman, outshone Andy Roberts, and the Lions won 2-1, which hurt greatly.

Confusingly, Ron Noades decided to bring in a proper manager, although Coppell and Lewington were still in place, but the decision to call for Dave Bassett wasn't universally celebrated. "Harry" Bassett had pitched up as the new manager at Palace a dozen years earlier, having had strong connections to Noades at Wimbledon, but, famously, he changed his mind after only a few days, and we ended up with Steve Coppell instead. This time Bassett seemed to relish the challenge of doing something with a team in transition, but with some obvious potential and ambition, and nobody can deny that he made a difference.

He managed to offload Gareth Taylor to his former club Sheffield United, and brought two journeymen in the other direction, defender David Tuttle and Australian Carl Veart. The goals started to flow from Freedman, Dyer and Ndah, but more importantly Nigel Martyn's form picked up and the defence started to look more and more secure, with clean sheets becoming the norm. Almost unnoticed, Palace went on a wonderful run of form which meant that by the time of the return match at Millwall at the end of March, they were sitting in third place, and starting to get serious about promotion. A most unlikely

ANDY ROBERTS

scorer that afternoon was defender Kenny Brown, on loan from West Ham, and Ndah's second on the way to a 4-1 win, a weak speculative overhead kick squirming embarrassingly out of Kasey Keller's fingers into the net, was indicative of the fact that luck was going Palace's way. The trio of Scots, Houghton, Freedman and Hopkin, were all in their best form of the season, and although the automatic promotion spot proved beyond them, Palace ended the season in third place, a real achievement for a team in such a constant state of flux, and for Dave Bassett as manager.

The play-off semi-final matched Palace with Charlton at the Valley, and the first leg didn't start well when Norwegian defender Leif Andersen made his most memorable contribution in a Palace shirt with an inexplicable diving bullet header at his own keeper. Martyn could only parry it, and Charlton's Shaun Newton followed up to

LEIF ANDERSEN

score, but Kenny Brown equalised with a belter before Carl Veart stooped to knock in the winner after George Ndah had attempted another spectacular overhead shot. Ndah was again instrumental in creating the only goal in the second leg for Ray Houghton, and Palace were back at Wembley once again, for the final against Martin O'Neill's Leicester City.

Just queuing for tickets at Selhurst Park the following weekend was an epic struggle itself, and unusually farcical even for Palace, but the sun was shining and there was a real mood of optimism as there was a sense that the fates were with us, and we were heading for a most unlikely promotion party. The game itself was very tense and cagey from both sides, but Andy Roberts made a rare advance to the edge of the opposition box to score his first ever Palace goal early on, and Leicester came back with a penalty after a clumsy lunge by Marc Edworthy. On balance, Leicester perhaps looked the better side, but the game went to extra time, and for the whole of the added 30 minutes

it just seemed inevitable that we would have the excitement of a penalty shootout.

I love the drama of penalties, and if we could have had them at Wembley in 1990 we might have won the FA Cup rather than enduring the trudge back to North West London on a midweek evening for a desperately disappointing replay. This time, with the kind of luck we'd been having in games, I was almost pleased that we didn't score a winner in normal time. With the game about to end, Leicester prepared for the shootout by bringing on the giant substitute goalkeeper, Zeljko Kalac, all six foot seven inches of him, and he took his place in goal in front of the Palace end. This was going to be fun, and that was all I was thinking as Leicester lumped the ball up the far end, Palace failed to clear, and Steve Claridge swung hopefully at the awkwardly bouncing loose ball. With his shin. Martyn never moved, and Claridge, briefly on Palace's books in the 80s, had sealed his place in Foxes' folklore forever to put them back into the Premier League a year after they had come down with Palace. As Martyn stood bemused on his line, he was surely thinking "maybe it's time to move on..."

1996-97

"...walking along, singing a song, walking in a Dougie wonderland"

After a relatively uncontroversial and placid year, the first for many seasons, it looked like we could expect more of the same, another season of "consolidation", or put another way, low expectations. The summer transfer activity certainly pointed that way: Nigel Martyn, after perhaps too many years' loyalty to Palace, moved to Leeds United and was back in the England frame, while Dave Bassett made a move for Sheffield United keeper Simon Tracey, who he knew well. The transfer got as far as Tracey having a medical at Selhurst Park, but after the deal broke down, Ron Noades slated Tracey in public for his "exorbitant" wage demands, and settled for Tottenham's well regarded reserve keeper Chris Day instead. Jamie Vincent had shown promise at left back following Dean Gordon's injury problems the previous season, but with Vincent moving to Bournemouth, that position was filled by Australian Kevin Muscat, who joined his compatriot Carl Veart in South London. Around the same time, Palace gave a trial to another young Australian centre-back, Tony Popovic, but for now that came to nothing.

Again the fans were calling for a true target man up front, but Dave Bassett persisted with Bruce Dyer to partner Freedman, and Palace made an unremarkable start to the new season. Dyer had shone for the England Under-21s, but despite his undoubted strength and speed, there was something missing from his game at club level, although this was by far his best season for Palace, ending it as top scorer. Dyer's England involvement, and that of Chris Day, together with Houghton's selection for the Republic of Ireland, meant some early disruption to the line-up, and goalkeeper Bobby Mimms came in for his one and only game for the third match of the season, at Huddersfield. Dougie Freedman got off the mark as Palace drew 1-1, but during that game Darren Pitcher was badly injured, and certain to miss the rest of the season. As it turned out, Pitcher never really recovered despite playing briefly for Orient later on, and tried unsuccessfully to sue Huddersfield for the tackle that ended his career. Players such as Pitcher and Muscat, wholehearted in the team's cause, or savages, depending on your point of view, were never really taken to the bosom of the home fans, and far more to my taste was David Hopkin, a natural leader who combined uncompromising battling qualities, in keeping with his appearance, with great creative flair and an eye for half a chance at goal.

DAVE BASSETT

The real news concerned speculation that Dave Bassett would take over at Manchester City, following the sacking of Alan Ball as manager. City had been relegated from the Premier League, but came to Selhurst Park in September still parading some big names, Uwe Rosler, Nigel Clough and the great Georgi Kinkladze among them. At the time, the assumption was that Bassett would be certain to take the job offered to him by Francis Lee, but perhaps Palace's superiority that day convinced the manager to stay, despite the idea of having big money to spend at City. Two fine goals from Hopkin and a pretty lucky one from Leif

Andersen put Palace in command before Dougie Freedman raced through on goal and was brought down by Kit Symons, denying him the chance to extend the lead to 4-0. That game finished 3-1 and Palace then started scoring for fun, 6-1 against Reading, despite Roberts' red card, another 6-1 against Southend, and seven goals over two legs in the league Cup against Bury. The goals were being shared out by players in all positions, but despite this purple patch there was still a perceived need for a target man, and for a while it appeared that Mark Bright would be returning on loan, before Sheffield Wednesday demanded a cash sale instead. The player who eventually came

NEIL SHIPPERLEY

in was 22-year-old Neil Shipperley, who looked the part, and was Palace's first big, strong - and slightly slow - centre forward since Iain Dowie. He struck up a good partnership with Freedman, and Dougie had by now come to the attention of Scotland manager Craig Brown, who put him on the bench for a World Cup qualifier game against Estonia in Tallinn. Scotland kicked off, but the opposition hadn't arrived because of a dispute about the time of the game, and Freedman played no part as the referee called the game to a halt, the Scots fans singing "...there's only one team in Tallinn".

The other remarkable story was that Steve Coppell, still Technical Director at Palace, having been talked of as successor to the recently sacked Ray Wilkins at QPR, then accepted the job at Manchester City that Bassett had turned down. It didn't seem right at the time, and Coppell only stayed at Maine Road just over a month before resigning, bravely facing up to the reality that he couldn't cope with the pressures of that particular job.

ANDY LINIGHAN

By November, Palace were up to second place in the table, but there were a few rather worrying and unpleasant undercurrents. There had been a mass brawl on the pitch during the home defeat to Swindon, and then again at Norwich, during which game Houghton and Muscat were sent off, and both clubs were later fined by the FA. A home defeat to Sheffield United particularly incensed Dave Bassett, and he made his thoughts crystal clear: "We were negative, we played without passion, we were lacking in enthusiasm, we looked frightened and quite simply, we bottled it... At the end of the day players wearing our shirts didn't want the ball, didn't pass the ball, and I will even go to the extent of saying that they went hiding." Things were starting to slip, and the defence was looking shaky despite Dean Gordon returning from injury, but improved with the arrival of former Arsenal centre-back Andy Linighan, signalling the end of Leif Andersen's undistinguished career in England. Reserve goalkeeper Carlo Nash earned rave reviews when he stood in for Chris Day against QPR, and kept his place in goal, but Palace continued to look as though they didn't really want another go at the play-offs this year.

Having turned down Manchester City earlier in the season, citing his desire to see things through at Palace, Dave Bassett shocked everyone when he suddenly left for Nottingham Forest in February, perhaps echoing the fans' own suspicions that their club was treading water, and heading for another disappointing end to the season. All in all it was looking a bit drab, with functional players like Veart and Tuttle regulars in the side, and a whole host of clubs lurking, ready to replace Palace in the top six. Even when there was yet another unexpected twist, Steve Coppell being reappointed as caretaker manager, it felt as if he was a stopgap to see out the season quietly. As late as mid-April, Coppell's side were down to ninth position, albeit with a game or two in hand, but somehow - following a dismal 3-0 defeat at Sheffield United - three wins from four games and a loss of nerve by Port Vale meant that Palace scraped into the play-offs in sixth place, with a game to spare. Curiously, Dougie Freedman had lost his place in the starting eleven, but came back for the final home game against Port Vale, and pointlessly got himself sent off for punching an opponent, meaning that he would miss the Wembley final should Palace get that far. It was completely out of character for Freedman, but seemed to fit with the theme of Palace's indiscipline throughout the season.

A year before, the semi-final against Charlton had seemed almost an entitlement, but this time it felt nervy from the start, the first leg against Wolves coming at home, where Palace had largely struggled. Furthermore, Geoff Thomas and Simon Osborn were in the Wolves side, and we had come to expect ex-players to score against Palace as a matter of course. Neil Shipperley's headed goal was the difference between the two sides until two minutes from the end, when substitute Dougie Freedman scored a sublime volleyed chip from distance to double the lead. Wolves immediately hit back through Jamie Smith for 2-1, which would have been a very fragile lead to take to the return leg, but once again Freedman scored the coolest of goals in the dying seconds, among the most important he would score for Palace, and the last for some while. Wolves did win the second leg 2-1, but never had the advantage after David Hopkin's magnificently emphatic equaliser, and we had yet another date at Wembley, this time on a sweltering hot day against Sheffield United.

STEVE COPPELL

Perhaps because of the glorious sunshine, the day felt more joyous from the very start than the Leicester game had a year earlier, and as tightly fought as the game was Palace always had the edge, although goal chances for either side were scarce. The five man defence, with Edworthy outstanding as sweeper, dealt with what little the Blades offered, but still the game seemed to be heading towards extra time, with the heat draining the players' energy. The clock was just ticking around to 90 minutes when David Hopkin picked up a loose clearance outside the opposition box, with virtually every other player between him and the goal. It was fitting that he should curl the ball so exquisitely past Simon Tracey in goal from distance, and it capped a superb season for Hopkin during which he had scored a fair few similar goals, taken over the captaincy, forced his way into the Scotland squad and into the thoughts of various acquisitive Premiership clubs. Delirium followed, although it was hard not to feel for the Sheffield fans having to suffer the same fate as we had against Leicester. Steve Coppell, although generous in acknowledging the part that Dave Bassett had played, had won promotion again in what had been a very difficult year for him, although in his usual downbeat way he admitted to slightly dreading what was ahead.

1997-98

"This penalty from Zohar to give Palace their first home win of the season..."

Lombardo, Zohar, Padovano, Brolin, Curcic, Goldberg... How do I start to make sense of this insane season? With Lombardo, I suppose. The fans had bitter memories of Palace's previous short-lived stay in the Premier League, and it was generally accepted that they came straight down because Ron Noades wouldn't invest big money to strengthen the side. Hence when a new director, Mark Goldberg, joined the board and pledged money to help seal Palace's place in the elite, Noades let him have his head, and went along with the audacious signing of Juventus and Italy star Attilio Lombardo, affectionately known as "Popeye", and soon to be renamed "The Bald Eagle". This was beyond anything we had known before at Palace, and was by far the most exciting signing in our history. Although Lombardo was just past his prime in Serie A, he still oozed quality, and it almost didn't matter that we had lost our talisman, and arguably our best player, David Hopkin, who had jumped ship to Leeds United. The transfer news just kept coming; Paul Warhurst from Blackburn, Watford keeper Kevin Miller, Icelandic defender Hermann Hreidarsson, unknown Scot Jamie Fullarton, and even Ray Wilkins returning as a coach.

Ray Houghton had worked his socks off in the First Division, but wouldn't have had the legs for a tough season at the top level, so he moved to Reading. Nevertheless, it looked a decent Palace side that faced Everton at Goodison to open the season. It looked even better after Lombardo and Dyer scored in a 2-1 victory, with stalwarts Dean Gordon and Simon Rodger in the line up alongside new skipper Roberts, and Warhurst coming in as a striker ahead of Shipperley and Freedman. Dyer had

enjoyed his best season yet during the promotion run, so kept his place up front, with high expectations. Palace were also on the trail of another overseas player, Israel's Itzik Zohar, who eventually came with a reputation as a dead-ball specialist.

HERMANN HREIDARSSON

A patchy first couple of months of the season saw Palace at least holding their own in the middle reaches of the table, with Lombardo the undoubted star and a wonderful influence on the players around him, but injuries started to play a part when David Tuttle limped off during a win against Wimbledon, the away leg of the Selhurst Park double-header.

Neil Shipperley forced his way back into the side after "losing weight and adjusting his lifestyle", but Dougie Freedman found himself down the pecking order once again, and was never given a real chance to have a go in the Premiership, which ranks as the first of Steve Coppell's many errors of judgement during the season. Kevin Muscat had also become something of a fringe player, with Fullarton preferred, and he and Freedman went to Wolves in a swap deal for right back Jamie Smith. I would have said that was the worst transfer business of the season, were it not for the £2 million paid for Wolves defender Neil Emblen, who returned to Molineux a few months later at a big loss. By late November George Ndah had gone to Swindon in search of first team football, and another expensive and slightly over the hill Juventus player arrived, the hugely disappointing Michele Padovano. Padovano made his debut at White Hart Lane, and Palace deservedly won 1-0, giving them their fifth away win of the season, and the best away record in the Premiership. The flip side, though, was that they could not win a home game for love nor money, and once Lombardo was injured, they began to slide slowly down the table, eventually going into free-fall with a run of eight straight defeats as they went into 1998.

With constant speculation about Mark Goldberg's plans to take over the club, Ron Noades revealed the terms of the sale. Goldberg was to pay £3 million pounds up front, which Noades claimed would be used to fund the Padovano deal, and Noades would give him until February 25th to come up with the rest of the £30 million asking price. Meanwhile, Goldberg appeared to be calling the shots regarding the comings and goings of players, and enticed the unhappy and unfit Swedish international Tomas Brolin, who had been a massive failure at Leeds. Brolin turned up almost out of nowhere to make a start against Everton, and put in his one decent performance in a Palace shirt to win a contract for the remainder of the season, during which time his contribution was minimal. Naturally, Palace lost against Everton to maintain their dreadful home record, but the hoodoo could have been broken in the previous game at Selhurst, on Boxing Day against Southampton. With the score at 1-1, Itzik Zohar came on as a substitute for Shipperley, and was no great shakes, wandering around as he had done on his previous few unremarkable appearances. When Bruce Dyer was brought down in the box, Zohar

made a show of grabbing the ball ahead of Dyer and insisted on taking the penalty. Let us be charitable and assume that Steve Coppell's account - that Dyer had hurt his ankle - is accurate, but let us also remember that Dean Gordon was on the pitch, a veteran taker of unstoppable penalties by this time. Zohar shot feebly, the keeper saved it, we didn't win, and that was the last we saw of the £1.2million Israeli.

MARCUS BENT

Both Lombardo and Padovano had flown home to Italy over the Christmas period and both Warhurst and Shipperley were out for lengthy periods as Palace tumbled towards relegation, with a wretched home defeat to Wimbledon perhaps the nadir. All the while, Goldberg's attempted takeover rumbled on and on, with more players coming and going. Andy Roberts, who had admittedly had a poor season, switched to Wimbledon, and Carl Veart and Welsh defender Gareth Davis had become surplus to requirements, but in came Valerian Ismael, Marcus Bent, Patrice Billio, Matt Jansen, and finally Sasa Curcic. Ismael was Palace's most expensive signing, at £2.75 million, but frankly we would have been better off with a fit Tuttle. Billio came and went within a few weeks, but Jansen was to prove the find of the season. He reportedly turned down interest from Manchester United to come to Palace from Carlisle, and scored a wonderful individual goal against Villa. However, it was already clear to everyone that Coppell, whether because of the boardroom shenanigans, interference from his masters, or his own inability to stick to a plan, had lost it.

PAUL WARHURST

As if Palace hadn't already become a laughing stock, it became common knowledge that Goldberg was lining up Terry Venables to take over following relegation, as well as attempting to get Paul Gascoigne in on loan, but in the meantime he put Lombardo in charge of team affairs with Brolin acting as interpreter, since Popeye's English was minimal. As Ron Noades tells it, this was done behind his back while he was on holiday, but the deed was done and Steve Coppell reverted to Director of Football. Lombardo's great achievement was to finally win a home game, against Derby, but once relegation was assured he reverted to his playing role, and the final embarrassment for the fans came when Ron Noades picked the team for the final three games. Of all the recent relegations, this one was the worst, an abject season with no excuses, and mayhem entirely of Palace's own making. Horrible luck with injuries had played a part, for sure, but a series of dreadfully misjudged and highly expensive purchases had been

their undoing, and the season's top scorer, Neil Shipperley, had managed a measly seven goals. Nevertheless, for some, there was a lot to look forward to; Goldberg would be investing fortunes, perhaps Lombardo was even staying, and Venables was coming back. For me, there wasn't a lot to look forward to; Venables was coming back.

1998-99

"Palace was my first club as a manager and now I think it could be my last."

Let's be fair to Venables. Let's put aside the way he left Palace and took half the team with him to QPR in 1980; let's put aside his sacking as Chief Executive of Tottenham and the parlous mess he left at Portsmouth; let's even put aside his ban from being a company director after the Department of Trade & Industry described his conduct in business as "such as to make him unfit to be concerned in any way with the management of a company." We must put all that aside in order to understand what on earth Mark Goldberg was thinking when inviting such an unctuous spiv to lead up his "Five Year Plan" for Crystal Palace, a plan which was to culminate in Palace becoming "a major force in Europe." Clearly, Goldberg had been taken in - as have so many before and since - by the myth of Venables' tactical brilliance on the pitch. Nobody believed this more than Venables himself, and with a compliant press corps in his back pocket, he was able to sidestep the inconvenient truths about his record of relative failure over the years with his reputation intact. Goldberg was blinded by the idea of landing someone apparently at the very top of his profession, and it seemed that money was no object. It was reported later that it cost Goldberg £135,000 even to enter into discussions with Venables, and that was just the beginning of what proved an extremely costly series of mistakes by the new owner.

Surprisingly, given Goldberg's grand plans, as the new season approached there appeared to be a remarkable level of continuity, with Steve Coppell staying as Director of Football, star players such as Lombardo, Curcic and Matt Jansen pledging themselves to the cause despite interest from Premiership clubs, and stalwarts like Simon Rodger, Bruce Dyer and Neil Shipperley still on the scene. However, in the background there was feverish activity, and Venables was explicit in his desire to build a large squad of players, with early transfers in for Dean Austin, Fraser Digby, Nicky Rizzo and David Amsalem. Also trumpeted were two other new arrivals, stars of the Argentina under-21s, Pablo Rodrigues and Cristian Ledesma. Dean Gordon did well to earn himself a Premiership contract at Middlesbrough, and poor Carlo Nash, who never got a look in once Kevin Miller arrived, started to rebuild his career at Stockport.

For Palace's first venture into European competition since the Anglo-Italian Tournament, they had entered the Intertoto Cup as England's sole representative, which might have offered a route to the UEFA Cup. Despite no enthusiasm from the new management, and with Terry Fenwick in charge whilst Venables completed his media commitments, a large crowd turned out to see Palace lose the first game against Turkey's Samsunspor, delaying the kick off because the club had severely underestimated the level of interest. Some then even travelled to the Black Sea port of Samsun for the away leg, to see Palace lose again in scorching heat, with the players not even acknowledging the effort that the fans had made to support them. Given the number of new signings, it was a little surprising to see so many youth team players taking part, such as Tony Folan, Steve Thomson, Hayden Mullins and striker Clinton Morrison, who had made a great impact and scored a last minute winner on his debut at the fag end of the previous season.

That brief flirtation with European glory out of the way, there was great anticipation ahead of the opening fixture against Bolton, but it was surprisingly familiar line-up that drew 2-2, with Austin and Mullins the only newcomers to the first team. It only took a couple of weeks for the cracks to start appearing, beginning with Marc Edworthy's departure to Coventry after he had been frozen out of the team. Still more players were arriving, among them Australian Craig Foster from Venables' previous club Portsmouth, two Chinese players, Fan Zhiyi and Sun Jihai, and a third Argentinian, Walter del Rio, instead of Rodrigues and Ledesma, who had mysteriously disappeared back to South America without kicking a ball for Palace. Early results were mediocre to poor, but a portent of the troubles ahead came when Neil Shipperley was unexpectedly sold to Dave Bassett's Nottingham Forest. The loss of Shipperley prompted Venables to reveal that "I did not want the player to go. However, Mark Goldberg had explained to me the temporary financial position which at the present time is making things very difficult for everybody including Mark himself. There is no problem between Mark and myself, in fact we get on very well together..." The cracks were

MATT SVENSSON

widening by mid-September, and when the promising Herman Hreidarsson left just as unexpectedly, the revolving door just kept on spinning: in came Matt Svensson, Craig Moore, Lee Bradbury and Gordan Petric, out went Bruce Dyer, Valerian Ismael,

Michele Padovano, and Paul Warhurst. It wasn't November yet, but Venables had already used 27 outfield players in the first 13 games of the season, and Palace had stayed resolutely at the tail end of the division.

There were some positives to take from the first third of the season, not least the potential of Fan Zhiyi and Sun Jihai before departing to the Asian Games for over a month, and Matt Jansen was continuing to show that he was destined for greater things, but Curcic started to fade from view, and newcomers such as Amsalem, Rizzo, Foster and Bradbury were massively disappointing. In stark contrast to the previous season, a run of six straight home wins balanced out the shocking away form, and the fans perhaps started to believe that Venables was getting it right, although Palace were still in no danger of troubling the top half of the table. As the year drew to a close, the media continued to focus on financial problems at Palace, with Ron Noades suing Goldberg, and on rumours that Curcic and Jansen wanted to leave, but in the programme for the QPR game just before Christmas, Goldberg was quick to pour scorn on such talk, and reaffirm that everything was hunky dory: "Behind the scenes my staff have been through the infrastructure, finances and all operations of the club, and are bringing everything into line with the five year plan I set in place last summer. In terms of football, I am proud to have assembled one of the strongest management teams in the country, and a squad who, over the five years, will take this club to heights it has never experienced before." What a fantasist Goldberg turned out to be; that was to be Jansen's final home game for Palace, and by mid-January both he and Venables had gone, along with Attilio Lombardo.

However bad we all thought things had become, they turned out to be much worse, and with each passing week the truth began to reveal itself. The departure of Venables and his coaching staff, as well as that of Lombardo, was meant to save on wages, and the fee for Jansen was reported to be over £4 million, yet soon it became clear that players and other staff weren't being paid, and the club somehow found itself in huge debt.

Steve Coppell once again stepped in as manager, and by early March Goldberg had no choice but to take the club into voluntary administration. The administrators quickly established that Palace's debts amounted to £22 million, with a cash flow shortage of an astonishing £500,000 a month, and soon any player who could be sold or sent on loan was out of the door. Lee Bradbury, David Tuttle, Jamie Fullarton, Andy Linighan and Jamie Smith all left within days of each other, as did Sasa Curcic, sadly. Curcic had been a huge favourite with the fans, and

SASA CURCIC

could turn a game with a flash of brilliance, or famously with a theatrical dive which won a penalty against Watford, but Steve Coppell was candid - as candid as he could be - about the reason that he wasn't being selected for much of the season: that he couldn't be bothered to train or play in

the reserves, so was never really fit. The last we saw of Sasa at Selhurst Park was when he carried a placard around the pitch protesting against the NATO bombing of Belgrade, where his family and that of Gordan Petric still lived, and of all the players who came and went over those bizarre two seasons at the end of the 90's, Curcic was the one who I would have loved to have seen much more of, along with Lombardo.

GORDAN PETRIC

It wasn't only the players who didn't know if and when they would be paid, and on April Fools' Day 1999, 46 members of staff were made redundant, many after years of service to the club. A few days later, the programme for the home game against Sunderland carried another page of upbeat twaddle from Goldberg, interviewed by the Publications Manager Pete King who, by then, had also found himself out of a job as a direct result of Goldberg's ineptitude. King's view of Goldberg is hard to argue with: "As far as I'm concerned the worst thing ever to happen in the history of Palace was Goldberg. Until he is out of the picture, Crystal Palace will go nowhere and achieve nothing."

With such a massive haemorrhaging of players, and after a run of eight games without a win, the task of keeping Palace from relegation should have been impossible, as Coppell was forced to rely on a growing number of youth team players, some of whom had hardly been heard of before. Leon MacKenzie, David Woozley, Andrew Martin, Andy Frampton, Sagi Burton, Wayne Carlisle, Gareth Graham and Stephen Evans were among those who played their part, and although none of them went on to long Palace careers, they all deserve our everlasting gratitude for saving Palace in those dark days. Somehow the team were galvanised to grind out unlikely results, typified by a 1-0 win at Norwich which sealed the previously unpopular Dean Austin's place in Palace folklore for his winning header in a game which some thought may have been Palace's last before extinction. A run of ten games unbeaten sent Palace as high as ninth in the table, safe from relegation with a handful of games left. The real finds of the season had been Hayden Mullins and Clinton Morrison, who ended up as top scorer just a year after making his debut, and who didn't cost a bean.

So who was to blame for the whole disaster? Certainly, Goldberg demonstrated monumental stupidity for getting into bed with Venables, Tel did what comes naturally in wanting a share of what he thought were Goldberg's millions, and Ron Noades stood back and let the whole thing happen in the first place, spotting early on how a fool and his money are soon parted. Who's to blame? The whole shabby, venal bunch.

1999-2000

"Maybe we can keep that Ashley Cole..."

Far from being a quiet summer, Palace's dire straits were as newsworthy as ever, as details emerged of the money owed to creditors, including Ron Noades and Terry Venables, as well as to players and other football clubs, including Strasbourg and Juventus. The lid was lifted on the extortionate contract, new house and car secured by Venables, as well as the amounts squandered on some very ordinary players, and it became ever clearer that Goldberg had really never come close to being able to secure the funds that he claimed in order to buy the club. The original firm of administrators had withdrawn, to be replaced by Simon Paterson, and there was much talk of a number of rival consortia bidding to become the new owners. One of these groups was apparently linked to Ron Noades, who had spent the past year running Brentford, and who still effectively owned Selhurst Park, but in pole position appeared to be a "City consortium", which turned out to be a front for Goldberg himself. Fortunately, Goldberg was by now facing personal bankruptcy, and the bid came to nothing, yet somehow Paterson was able to convince the Football League that Palace would be able to fulfil the fixtures for the season ahead, and by the start of the season Mark Goldberg had been forced to resign as chairman, to be replaced by long-standing director Peter Morley.

Goldberg's departure was greeted with delight by the fans, who had shown their solidarity by organising a comedy night at the Fairfield Halls to raise funds for those made redundant. "Glad All Over" featured acts from celebrity fans Kevin Day, Jo Brand, Sean Hughes and the wonderful Eddie Izzard, as well as the sympathetic Hammers fan Phil Jupitus, with auctions of items donated by several ex-players, including Geoff Thomas and Nigel Martyn, raising over £15,000. Further proof of the determination of fans to get involved in rescuing their beloved club was the launch of what was to become the Crystal Palace Supporters' Trust, which succeeded in raising over £1million in loans, with a view to becoming part of any potential rescue package, and giving the fans a presence on the board. The Trust were lucky enough to have the full support of Steve Coppell, and the response of the fans gave us all a great collective hope that the club would somehow survive.

SIMON RODGER

There wasn't a lot to be upbeat about on the pitch, though, and before the season had even started, a lucrative tour of China was soured somewhat by the news that Sun Jihai wouldn't be coming back to South London. Clearly no new players could be bought, so the squad started the season with a very threadbare look to it. It was hard to make a convincing case for the season to be anything but a dour battle against relegation, with so many young players in the team. With Kevin Miller having gone, and David Tuttle being sold after the first game, there was very little experience to fall back on. However, a thrilling 3-2 victory at Barnsley raised hopes temporarily, before a dreadful 7-1 mauling by Huddersfield confirmed what a long season this was going to become. Coppell picked his men up, though, and with the commitment of players like Simon Rodger, Andy Linighan and Fan Zhiyi, allied to at least some finesse from Hayden Mullins and Clinton Morrison, results began to improve, with again some terrific results at home. A 4-0 defeat of Portsmouth, Lee Bradbury's last

CLINTON MORRISON

Palace game before returning to Pompey, and a 3-0 win over QPR stood out, and despite losing Morrison for some months, Matt Svensson returned from injury to put together a good run of games for once, scoring freely and showing a bit of quality as well as power.

A couple of months into the season Steve Coppell started to busy himself in the loan market, and we saw glimpses of the Venezuelan, Fernando De Ornelas, and the Brazilian, Fumaca, both quickly forgotten, before Terry Phelan arrived from Manchester City. Phelan had been part of Wimbledon's famous cup-winning side in 1988, along with Eric Young and Andy Thorn, and had been close to signing for Palace at one point. His presence at left back gave the defence a bit more guile, but as Phelan's loan period ran out, Svensson decided to move to Charlton, Simon Rodger suffered another injury and results dipped again, with relegation remaining a distinct

possibility. Come March, though, Coppell brought in two more loan players who played a big part in the scrap for survival, Chelsea's Finnish striker Mikael Forssell and left back Ashley Cole from Chelsea. Forssell had come to England with a big reputation, and was very much being groomed for the future by Chelsea, but Ashley Cole hadn't yet got near the Arsenal first team, and was unheard of. As soon as he came to Palace, Cole's control, speed and ability to take the ball forward marked him out as a young player of real quality, and I wasn't alone among Palace fans in remarking that he would play for England one day, and wishing we could keep him. In a season that unsurprisingly lacked too much excitement, the quality of Forssell and Cole was some antidote to the continuing anxiety about the club's continued existence, and as the season wore on there was a

HAYDEN MULLINS

very real concern among fans that various mystery buyers had evaporated. We heard of an elusive figure called Gerry Lim, which we started to suspect was a pseudonym for Noades or Goldberg, but despite positive noises from the administrator, nothing seemed to materialise, and it started to look as if any deal may have been dependent on Palace avoiding relegation.

A poor run of six games, with only two points to show for them, left Palace going into the penultimate game of the season still in danger. Matt Jansen returned to his old stamping ground with a first half goal for Blackburn which left the Palace fans in a state of shock, and which he chose not to celebrate. Palace fought back in the second half against a Blackburn side whose season

CRAIG FOSTER

was well and truly over, and Ashley Cole marked a great performance with his one and only goal for Palace, a clever chip from just inside a crowded penalty area to equalise. Clinton Morrison then rounded off another excellent season for him with a headed winner, ensuring Palace's unlikely survival with a game remaining. Jansen confirmed his enduring reputation as one of the good guys of football when he stayed on the pitch to congratulate his former team mates after the final whistle. The season ended with a 2-1 victory at Tranmere, the goals fittingly coming from Morrison and Mullins, perhaps the club's two best players by now, and the final table showed Palace in 15th place, a startling eight points clear of relegation. Although there had been a few glimpses of flair, this had been a season of knuckling down and digging deep. Players such as Dean Austin, Andy Linighan, Wayne Carlisle, David Woozley, Steve Thompson, Craig Foster and Andrew Martin will never be counted among the most talented footballers in Palace's history, but there is no doubt that, with Steve Coppell's expert guidance, they had performed something close to a miracle.

2000-01

"Once he's properly fit, I'm sure Ruddock will show us his quality..."

Administrator Simon Paterson's quest to find a buyer for the club had dragged on for almost a year when it emerged that the enigmatic Mr Lim was indeed a real person, and that he had been trying to buy the club, but had then reached an agreement to sell it straight away to Simon Jordan, a name had not previously been widely touted. Jordan was another self-made millionaire with claims to being a lifelong Palace fan, who had made his fortune when selling his mobile phone business, and, in all honesty, the fans were just relieved that the club had been saved from going into liquidation, which had seemed highly possible. Never mind that he looked just the sort of person you would want to avoid doing any kind of business with; at least he wasn't Goldberg. His whole demeanour spoke of arrogance and vanity, and perhaps it was no surprise that he and Steve Coppell didn't see eye to eye from the start, and concluded that they couldn't work together. The premise for Coppell's shock departure before the summer had ended was a string of bad results in the pre-season friendlies, and losing 5-0 to Millwall was the final straw, but it isn't hard to see why the humble, intelligent and honest Coppell felt that there was an insurmountable clash of personalities.

With all the signs suggesting that Jordan was looking for a yes-man to come in as manager, it was a real surprise when he announced the appointment of Alan Smith, who Ron Noades had sacked following relegation five years earlier. The thinking was sound: Smith had won promotion to the Premiership in his first season as manager, and had a good reputation for working with young players, which was still the core of the Palace squad. Although he had been dismissed as manager at Wycombe Wanderers, Smith had spent a couple of years in charge of Fulham's youth academy, and above all was perceived as the anti-Noades candidate, having fallen out with him in style during the relegation season. Perhaps Simon Jordan wanted to curry favour with the large number of fans who still felt bitter about Noades' part in Palace's descent into near oblivion, or perhaps he really had considered several strong candidates and concluded that Alan Smith was the best man for the job. Either way, it was obvious that he wasn't getting his yes-man, and I was probably in a fairly small minority in anticipating that Smith would do a great job.

SIMON JORDAN

Despite the Supporters' Trust having had a part to play in bringing Gerry Lim and Jordan together in the first place, the new owner decided that he didn't want them buying a stake in the club or being represented at Board level, which set the sidewinding tone for Jordan's reign, so the Trust decided to offer to repay everyone who had lent money to help save their club. Jordan had been offered a golden opportunity to build real bridges with the fans, and to get them on his side, but from the very start that never really happened, and although grateful that he came along when he did, from then on there was never any real warmth towards him.

With Ashley Cole having played himself into Arsenal's first team reckoning with his performances at Selhurst Park, he was clearly out of reach, but Palace did pick up two other young Arsenal reserves in Tommy Black and Julian Gray, as well as goalkeeper Stuart Taylor on loan for the start of the season. A new left back was a priority, and the position was filled by Middlesbrough's Craig Harrison, but the two headline signings for the start of the new campaign were Jamie Pollock and Neil Ruddock. Pollock had been an impressively skilful player for Middlesbrough in past encounters with Palace, but already his best days were well behind him at the age of 26, and he was renowned for scoring a wonderful own goal for Manchester City which had consigned them to relegation. If Pollock looked unfit and overweight, that was nothing compared to Ruddock, who revelled in his reputation as a villain, and who had long since conceded defeat in the battle against the bulge.

NEIL RUDDOCK

Very little went right early on for Smith although games were being lost only narrowly; there were signs of promise from Black and Gray, and Morrison's first goal of the season, a cool finish in the first minute to defeat Barnsley, seemed to signal better times ahead. Instead, a sequence of six defeats on the spin culminated in a home defeat at the hands of Grimsby, which prompted ever louder calls for Alan Smith to be given the boot, and following which Simon Jordan was moved to storm into the dressing room to bawl out the players. Smith pointed the finger at the players in no uncertain terms: "I think the players really need to look at themselves. I had all 16 of them in the dressing room for one-and-a-half hours and only four of them had anything to say and two of them are on loan, that says it all. Someone said that they were giving their all but if that is their best I'd hate to see what their worst is… If these attitudes don't change, it will be anarchy and you'll have the lunatics running the asylum… I feel like Michael Caine in Zulu. A pistol in my hand, 16,000 coming over the hill trying to claim my head… I can't shoot all of them so I might as well shoot the three fellas nearest me who are causing all of the problems. I think our players live in cloud cuckoo land… The bottom line is 'have we got any balls?' and the answer is 'no we haven't'." Morrison and Mullins, Palace's most consistent players the previous year, were placed on the transfer list with Jamie Smith, and it looked like the season was heading for disaster.

Perhaps it was Alan Smith's rant that did the trick, or perhaps it was the surprise and welcome return of Dougie Freedman, who had been frozen out by David Platt at Nottingham Forest, and the arrival of Steve Staunton on loan, but Palace immediately embarked on their best run of results for some time, remaining unbeaten in eleven league and cup games. Freedman and Clinton Morrison immediately struck a rich vein of goals and new Latvian signing Andrejs Rubins hit a cracking goal from distance in the 3-0 League Cup win over Leicester. A 2-1 victory over Sunderland, with a brilliant effort from Morrison, sent Palace into the League Cup semi-final, the first time Palace had enjoyed any Cup success of note for six barren years. The semi-final pitted Palace against Liverpool over two legs, and the home leg on a Wednesday night in January proved well worth the wait, with Rubins scoring another stunner with his left foot, and Palace winning 2-1 in front of a near capacity crowd. Clinton Morrison was quick to offer his analysis of Liverpool's shortcomings: "Heskey missed a few and Owen missed a few. On a better day they would have put them away. But I was thinking, I wish I had some of the chances they had. I would have put at least two of them away." A few days later, Freedman was ecstatic to contribute one of Palace's three goals which beat Nottingham Forest at the City Ground, but Liverpool demolished Palace 5-0 in the second leg of the League Cup game, with Morrison's humiliating air shot in front of the Kop perhaps just deserts. With two thirds of the season gone Palace had climbed to what seemed a fairly acceptable mid-table position.

By now both Pollock and Ruddock had proved themselves unfit for the first team, in every sense, and various new loanees were tried, none of whom caught the eye as Palace started to tumble downwards, and towards Division Two. Matthew Upson, Amir Karik and Ricardo Fuller came and went before Palace finally made two proper signings to try and rescue their season, the Finnish International Aki Riihilahti, and the return of another former hero, Freedman's fellow Scot David Hopkin. In truth, neither made a huge impact at first, and couldn't halt the slide, so that with two games remaining, the relegation that had seemed unthinkable was looking almost certain. Simon Jordan belatedly sacked Alan Smith and replaced him with Steve Kember for the final two games, but although it seemed a pointless gesture,

plenty of us ventured down to Portsmouth for the midweek evening game, knowing that nothing less than victory would suffice, against a Pompey team also fighting for survival. Kember made a couple of bold changes to the side, bringing in Wayne Carlisle for Craig Harrison, and starting Steve Thomson and American defender Greg Berhalter, but crucially he chose to use Clinton Morrison in deep role behind Freedman and Forssell, which worked an absolute treat. The team played with a self-belief which we hadn't seen for a while, and

WAYNE CARLISLE

during the first half we were treated to goals from Forssell, Riihilahti and a trademark individual effort from Freedman, leaving us exhilarated at half time, with the score at 3-1. We hadn't had a great view of those goals from the far end of the ground, but Dougie made up for it with a casual header from Morrison's cross bang in front of us in the away end, and with the game ending 4-2, we knew that a victory at Stockport on the last day of the season would at least give Palace a mathematical chance of staying up.

The permutations at the bottom of the table were complex, with Palace, Portsmouth and Huddersfield all endangered, but what was clear was that we had to beat Stockport, who were already safe. I had a prior arrangement which meant that I had to drive from London to Devon on that Saturday afternoon, so I timed the journey to coincide with the radio commentary for the last two hours. The tension throughout wasn't conducive to safe driving, and I listened anxiously as Palace failed to score the goal they needed. The game wore on and I found myself arriving at my destination ahead of time, with five minutes of the match left. I parked up in a narrow street in a Devon village, to listen glumly on the radio to my beloved team's demise. I had parked just yards from the birthplace of John Lee, later to be known as John "Babbacombe" Lee, and later still as "The Man They Couldn't Hang". Sentenced to

footage of Steve Kember's reaction to the goal tells you all you need to know about his love for Crystal Palace, and in that sublime moment Dougie Freedman joined him in the pantheon of genuine Palace legends.

STEVE KEMBER

death for murder, Lee went to the gallows, but the trap failed three times, and he was spared. Three minutes remained when David Hopkin bundled the ball away from defence with more than a hint of handball and lumped it up to Morrison with his back to the defence. Dougie took the ball off Clinton's toes and headed for the box. A little feint to the left, a jink to the right, and he placed it perfectly past the keeper for the winner. The trapdoor could still have opened for Palace, as there was an agonising wait for the final whistle at Huddersfield, who would have sent Palace down if they had equalised against Birmingham, but luck was smiling on us that day. The TV

2001-02

"Steve is happy here and the chances of him ever going to St Andrews are a million-to-one against."

Whether it had been a stroke of genius, or simply great good luck on Simon Jordan's part to turn to Steve Kember, it had done the trick, and the players had responded magnificently. The question was, should Kember be given the job permanently, or indeed would he want it? Kember's place in the hearts of older Palace fans was already secure. He had been an outstanding young player for Palace in the promotion team of 1969, skippered the side in the old First Division before leaving for Chelsea, and had returned as the key player in Terry Venables' young promotion team of 1979. Ron Noades had given him a brief spell as manager in the gloom of the mid-eighties, between Dario Gradi and Alan Mullery, and he later returned to Selhurst Park as a coach during Alan Smith's first reign. Quite properly, Jordan told Kember that he had a "job for life" at Palace, which although not technically in the chairman's gift, was a gesture born of both gratitude and respect for the man. However, perhaps mindful of the mistake he had made in bringing back Alan Smith, Jordan decided to look elsewhere for a new manager, and very swiftly unveiled Steve Bruce, with Kember staying on as his assistant. Bruce had been in the Manchester United team that had eventually beaten Palace in the 1990 FA Cup final, and had already had short spells as manager at Sheffield United, Huddersfield, where he was sacked, and Wigan, who he had only joined seven weeks earlier.

Bruce had fallen out with Huddersfield, the chairman writing in a programme that he had "made a mistake by believing that a great footballer would make a great football manager". Nevertheless, at Wigan he had impressed the chairman Dave Whelan, who wanted to keep Bruce until Jordan made him "an offer he couldn't refuse". It was good that Jordan had acted decisively, and Bruce appeared to have an aura that convinced the sceptics that he was someone going places as a manager. He looked the sort of person who could certainly stand up to Jordan, and would share his evident ambition for the club, so on balance, despite Bruce's long association with Manchester United, it appeared to be a pretty good appointment.

STEVE BRUCE

The summer transfer targets failed to stir much excitement, and included Coventry's Australian striker John Aloisi, Middlesbrough's Andy Campbell, and Arjan Van De Zeeuw of Wigan, but none of these materialised. The only new faces turned out to be American international Jovan Kirovski and Australian Tony Popovic, followed soon after by Bradford City goalkeeper Matt Clarke. All in all, it was a pretty stable side that started the season, with Freedman and Morrison continuing their potent partnership up front and Fan Zhiyi and Dean Austin still at the back, and in the first game they came from 2-0 behind to beat Rotherham 3-2, Jamie Smith scoring a rare goal. Fan Zhiyi also started the second game, an early rematch with Stockport, and all went very smoothly in the 4-1 win, but that proved to be Fan's last game for Palace. There had been disquiet for some time about the time that Fan spent captaining his country, and once again he was needed for China's World Cup qualifying games, which necessitated some changes to the defence, and gave Bruce the opportunity to assess Popovic, Austin and Craig Harrison, as well as trying Matt Clarke in Kolinko's place. Three defeats followed, with eleven goals conceded, and after Steve Vickers arrived on loan from Middlesbrough, Bruce concluded that he could do without Fan, who, in his words "had let the club down after indicating when he signed his new contract that he would not be travelling to China." Yes, that was Steve Bruce, in his own words, taking the moral high ground on honouring contracts. Fan eventually ended up at Dundee United after helping China to qualify for the World Cup finals for the first time in their history, and Palace were left with a very big hole in their defence, which was never really plugged for the rest of the season.

Nevertheless, Bruce appeared to know what he was doing, and made good use of what players he had. Julian Gray started to excel down the left, Riihilahti continued to improve and become a fixture in midfield, and newcomer Jovan Kirovski added a bit of style alongside him. But most of all, it was the form of Dougie Freedman and Clinton Morrison that sent Palace up and up the table, with a run of seven straight wins, including a 5-0 demolition of Grimsby - sweet revenge for the woeful home defeat a year earlier - a joyous 4-1 win over Sheffield Wednesday, and 4-0 against Wimbledon. The reward for the two strikers came as they were called up for their respective countries. Dougie finally made his Scotland debut against Latvia, even scoring against his team mate Kolinko in goal, and South London boy Clinton Morrison was in the

lucky position of having a grandmother from Dublin, so became an Irishman, and later went on to win 36 caps, scoring 9 goals.

All was going extremely well, better than most people expected, and it looked as if Jordan had chosen his new manager very wisely. In mid-October, Trevor Francis left as manager of Birmingham, and there were mischievous rumours linking Bruce with the vacant job, but Jordan quickly scotched them: "Steve is happy here and the chances of him ever going to St Andrews are a million-to-one against. Steve has a three-year contract and there is no get-out clause." A 1-0 victory over Wolves saw Palace leapfrog them to take top position, but the Birmingham rumours wouldn't go away, and eventually Bruce tendered his resignation, although apparently there had been no official approach from Birmingham. Palace were all over the papers again, and Simon Jordan took out an injunction forcing Bruce to work his nine months' notice on "gardening leave", putting Steve Kember back in charge of the team, along with Terry Bullivant. Although compensation was eventually agreed with Birmingham, there was no doubt that, whatever Bruce's underlying reasons for leaving, Jordan had won the public relations war and claimed the moral high ground. His war of words with the then Birmingham owners has been fantastically entertaining over the years, and he has made great play of the fact that their wealth was accrued through pornography: "If I see another David Gold interview on the poor East End Jewish boy done good I'll impale myself on one of his dildos."

With the matter finally settled, and Bruce's reputation as Judas sealed, Palace's form dipped a little, but hope was restored when a new manager arrived to oversee a fine 2-1 victory over Manchester City. Trevor

Francis was to be the fifth manager to serve under Jordan in his 18 months at the club so far, if one counts Steve Coppell, and the sincere hope was that he would get it right this time. Francis had been a fabulous player for Birmingham, which led to Brian Clough signing him for Nottingham Forest, famously becoming Britain's first £1 million player. For Forest he scored the winning goal in the European Cup final, but as a manager his record had been no more than humdrum. He was sacked by Sheffield Wednesday before a spell at Birmingham characterised by consistently failing to win promotion out of Division One via the play-offs. It was hardly one to get the pulse racing, and there was a slight suspicion that Jordan was keen to get one over on Birmingham, who had given up on Francis so recently.

All too predictably, results continued to be patchy, and Palace settled into a zone familiar to Trevor Francis, on the fringes of the play-off positions, while trying to strengthen the defence with Christian Edwards, on loan, followed by permanent signings Kit Symons, Curtis Fleming and Danny Granville. None were especially bad players, but all fitted the mould of decent enough Division One journeymen, and the fans were kind of getting the point, that this was the limit of the club's ambition. What was needed was a big money signing, someone to make the headlines, and revitalise a season that was heading nowhere. £2.4million was big money, and Ade Akinbiyi certainly attracted headlines, but none of them good. Peter Taylor had made Akinbiyi Leicester's record signing when paying an astonishing £5.5million, and by any standards he had failed at Filbert Street, being cited as the main reason that Taylor was later sacked. He came to Palace with the nickname of Akinbadbuy already given to him by Leicester fans and the press,

and never showed the slightest glimpse of casting it off. Akinbiyi only scored twice before the season ended, and I actually saw his one home goal that year, a tap in against Preston giving him the chance at last to display his celebrated torso. I shall add it to that other treasured memory, Marco Gabbiadini's goal against Notts County ten years earlier.

ALEX KOLINKO

Finishing just in the top half of Division One was actually a pretty good achievement considering how recently the club had nearly gone out of business, and how close they had been to relegation, but it just felt a little disappointing after the season had promised so much under Steve Bruce, and it was also quite disconcerting to finish a season without the usual drama and trauma of relegation or promotion that we were accustomed to. There had been a lot to enjoy, not least Freedman and Morrison scoring 42 League goals between them, fine seasons for Julian Gray and Hayden Mullins, and an outstanding one for Aki Riihilahti, but was Trevor Francis the forceful and charismatic leader we needed to become promotion contenders next season? I didn't think so, but Simon Jordan must have done.

"Who needs Andy Johnson when we've got Tommy Black?"

Sometimes a new player will come into a team and make an instant impression, for good or bad, and sometimes they need more time to settle in and find their feet before flourishing. Of the four new signings that lined up for the opening game against Preston, it was the imposing centre-half Darren Powell who looked the best. Finding a decent partner for Popovic had been a huge problem for Trevor Francis, but Powell looked the part from the off, scored a goal on his debut, and was very soon being likened by fans to the mighty Eric Young. Danny Butterfield also looked comfortable at Division One level, having

DANNY BUTTERFIELD

signed from Grimsby, and Shaun Derry had arrived to beef up the midfield. There was another new starter, a short bald bloke called Andy Johnson, who was stretchered off with a suspected broken neck. Johnson had arrived as the makeweight in a deal that took Clinton Morrison to Birmingham for £4.5 million during the summer, which was an offer that Simon Jordan couldn't resist after Steve Bruce had irritatingly won promotion to the Premiership. Morrison was at his peak, and it was an ideal chance for him to play at the top level, but Johnson's move in the other direction seemed to

confirm that Palace were at a point where they were prepared to take cast-offs from a team like Birmingham.

As the team made a stuttering start, so did Johnson, and before long Francis had signed Dele Adebola for a bit of power up front, since Akinbiyi was likely to be out injured for several months. Johnson's first goal for Palace was tapped home from a yard against Plymouth in the League Cup, but despite his endeavour and evident pace, he didn't look the ideal partner for Freedman, and looked possibly better when played on the right wing. His speed and tenacity won a penalty for Freedman to score against Wolves, but for the first couple of months he was substituted more often than not, and I had certainly made my mind up about him. From what I had seen, pace was his only real asset, but he was too small to be an effective striker, and more to the point, didn't seem to know where the goal was. The season was beginning to pan out in a very predictable way for a Trevor Francis side, and apart from a 7-0 stroll past Cheltenham in the League Cup, the expectation for most games was yet another draw. The biggest drama was in the home draw against Bradford, when Francis was sent from the dugout after punching his own substitute keeper Kolinko, who he said was smirking after the opposition scored. The "away" fixture against ground sharers Wimbledon was meant to be the last before they moved to set up shop in Milton Keynes, and Andy Johnson finally got off the mark in the league with another tap-in, but the result was, again, a draw.

There are a few opposition teams that it is very important to beat, whereas others you can take or leave. For me, it's nice if we beat Aston Villa, but not essential, whereas a result against Wolves is vital. We've beaten Liverpool a few times, and it's always fun, but Everton are more satisfying. Charlton? Not really, but Millwall, absolutely. There's a logic to the long standing local rivalry with Millwall, if not to the others, but I've not met a Palace fan who doesn't get a very special feeling whenever we face Brighton. Although a relatively new phenomenon, dating back to Alan Mullery's days there in the 70's, the rivalry has become real and enduring, but the game against Brighton in October 2002 was special for a number of reasons. First of all, this was the first time in over a decade that the two sides had been in the same division, and with Brighton already stranded at the bottom of the table after losing eleven games in a row, it looked like being the last for a while. Secondly, it was a chance for the crowd to welcome back Simon Rodger, whose epic career at Palace had been terminated by Trevor Francis, and who had just signed for Brighton. But most of all, Brighton's manager that day was Steve Coppell, still worshipped by all at Selhurst Park, who gave him a rousing and emotional reception. With all of that, the most probable result was an uneventful draw, but this was to be the day that Andrew Johnson was reborn as AJ, a brand new Palace hero. He scored a toe-poke for 1-0 and a diving header for 2-0, then burst through into the box to win a penalty which Dougie put away for the third. Another powerful run into the box drew a foul from the defender, a red card, and another penalty which this time AJ claimed for his hat-trick. Julian Gray's splendid individual goal made it 5-0. Just so everyone is clear, that's Crystal Palace 5, Brighton and Hove Albion 0.

If AJ had disappeared from the first team after that game, he would still have been lauded forever, but the hat-trick transformed him, and with a new-found confidence he scored a second hat-trick only three days later, at Walsall. A stunning left-footed volley, a header, then a low right-footed shot to win the game 4-3 was followed by a goal at Ipswich and two against Coventry, which made it 10 goals in 5 games. I've never been so happy to be proved wrong about a player who I'd dismissed as pretty ordinary. I still didn't think much of Adebola, though, or Shaun Derry, for that matter.

SHAUN DERRY

Things were surely moving in the right direction, with Julian Gray impressing on the wing, young Wayne Routledge contributing some outstanding cameos, and Kolinko regaining his place in goal once again from Matt Clarke, but when Freedman was injured in November, and Johnson the following month, there was a worry about where the goals would come from. Adebola chipped in with a couple, but the revelation was Tommy Black, in and out of the side under Francis, and starting to look out of condition and surplus to requirements. His little spree of 9 goals in 8 games earned him a renewed contract, and saw Palace at last thinking seriously about the play-offs come the New Year.

However, the season's only remaining drama was confined to the FA Cup, with Palace drawn against Liverpool in the fourth round. Every few years Palace face Liverpool in one cup or another, and the ties are never dull, this being no exception. It was by no means a vintage Liverpool team at the time under Gerard Houllier, and although they were still in the upper reaches of the Premiership, they had a beatable look about them, which gave Palace confidence, along with AJ's recent return from injury. Both sides had chances to win, but the game finished goalless, the main incident being a serious injury to Chris Kirkland, which halted what was developing into a highly promising career as Liverpool's goalkeeper. It came after a burst of speed into the box from Dele Adebola, showing a rare change of pace to round a defender, but the Palace striker was utterly blameless for the collision which caused Kirkland's injury. Approaching the replay, it was difficult not to think back to the 5-0 drubbing at Anfield under Alan Smith, but this time Palace defended stoutly, and Julian Gray was the star of the show. A precise and powerful volley from Gray for the first goal was followed by an own goal from Gray's cross to win the tie at Anfield. What made the victory even sweeter was that Palace had achieved it with only ten men after Dougie Freedman was sent off for retaliation with 20 minutes remaining. The prize was a home tie in the fifth round against Leeds United.

When they came to Selhurst Park for the cup game, Leeds were a Premiership team just starting to deteriorate and head towards the relegation zone, and their manager was coming under increasing pressure. Indeed he was sacked a month after the Palace game, but for now Terry Venables knew that his welcome back to South London would be less than friendly. The boos for Venables before the game contrasted with the reception given to Steve Coppell earlier that season, and gave a pretty fair idea of their respective places in the hearts of Palace fans. How fitting that Venables

should be witness to daylight robbery, as Tommy Black's shot to give Palace the lead was not only handled by Michael Duberry, but was clearly over the line. Well over, massively over, obviously over the line to anyone with eyes. "Goal!" said the players. "Goal!" said the crowd. "No!" said the ref and linesman. "Thank you very much," said Venables, as Leeds won 2-1, and Palace's season dwindled to nothing.

TOMMY BLACK

For the first time since I'd been going to Selhurst Park, I found myself losing interest a little. Palace continued to win a couple, lose a couple and draw a few, but something about Trevor Francis just made me switch off for a time. I have no memory of the on-loan striker Noel Whelan scoring three goals, nor of David Hunt's two appearances. I barely recall Trevor Francis being sacked and Steve Kember taking charge for the rest of the season, and I vaguely remember a feeling of dread when Bryan Robson was touted as manager. There is something in the recesses of my memory, though, which proves that I was there: "that Ben Watson looks a good player".

bouncebackability, *n. chiefly sport: The capacity to recover quickly or fully from a setback, bad situation, etc.*

The collapse of ITV Digital in 2002, and the loss of £180million still owed to the clubs outside the Premiership, was starting to have the impact that many predicted and a dozen or more clubs had followed Palace's example and gone into some form of administration. One of these was Wimbledon, who under chairman Charles Koppel planned to move to Milton Keynes and set up as MK Dons, which was disgracefully sanctioned by the Football League. Having shared Selhurst Park since 1991, Wimbledon had planned to move to a hockey stadium in Milton Keynes until their new ground was finished, but as this was delayed, they were forced to start the season still sharing with Palace. In lieu of rent owed, Palace took back Neil Shipperley, who had still been playing and scoring regularly for the Dons, although when he appeared again in a Palace shirt he looked badly out of condition, bringing back memories of Jamie Pollock who Simon Jordan claimed to have sacked for being overweight. Palace were starting to tighten their belts as well, and high earners Ade Akinbiyi and Danny Granville were transfer-listed, with a likelihood that Hayden Mullins and Julian Gray would be on their way to bigger clubs. Gray had by now become highly unpopular with the fans, who picked up the clues in Jordan's reference to "big-time Charlies" at the club. Mullins' attitude however was unimpeachable, despite him running down his contract in the hope of a move.

In fact, Gray's planned deals with Leeds, Charlton and Blackburn fell through, because none thought that he was worth the fee that Palace wanted and he eventually went on loan to Cardiff. Granville didn't attract too much interest, and Akinbiyi proved very hard to shift until Stoke took him off Palace's hands for nothing, to Kember's great relief. One sad but inevitable departure was that of Alex Kolinko, now in dispute with Palace over claims of money owed, and Dele Adebola was released after an unremarkable year of effort but no great inspiration. Following a bitty season of injuries and loss of form, Aki Riihilahti's midfield place was threatened with the arrival of Michael Hughes, who had been kicking his heels for a year after a contract dispute between West Ham and Wimbledon.

MICHAEL HUGHES

Without too much fanfare, Steve Kember was kept on as manager, this time without the "caretaker" label, and vowed to get Palace playing the passing game, playing to the strengths of Freedman rather than the likes of Akinbiyi and Adebola. With that in mind, the decision to bring back Shipperley perhaps seemed an odd one, but it seemed to work. Dougie scored a hat-trick on the first day as Palace came from behind to beat Burnley, despite both Routledge and Derry being sent off. Two more wins followed and Kember had made a dream start to his latest stint in the hot seat, winning over some of the sceptics who, despite loving Kember for his devotion to Palace over the years, had misgivings about his credentials as a manager, and above all were desperate for him not to fail. From top of the table after three games, four games after that the doubts were starting to surface, with five players already sent off, and home defeats at the hands of Sheffield United ("Warnock can't help being a prat," said Kember afterwards) and Bradford City. Mullins finally got his move, not to a big club as expected, but to West Ham, and really, who could blame him? Slowly but surely, it all started to go a bit Trevor Francis, and by mid-October Palace were already sliding down into the bottom half of the table when they faced Ipswich in a midweek home game. When Andy Johnson and Dougie Freedman score three between them, you don't expect to get beaten, but Ipswich scored a late goal to win the game 4-3, a neat chip after dreadful defending, coming from the boot of big Ipswich striker Shefki Kuqi.

"Jordan Out" was becoming a pretty regular chant by now, but it was Steve Kember who was starting to fear for his job, as his team tumbled towards the relegation places. The Palace team that lined up against Wigan for a Saturday lunchtime televised game was one that should have been pushing for promotion from what was a quite ordinary Division One, but I could hardly believe what was unfolding on the screen as I supped my pint in a South London pub. Derry, Riihilahti, Freedman, Johnson, Butterfield, all good players, at times terrific players, plus Danny Granville returning from the wilderness, all played abysmally as Wigan strolled to 5-0. It was the single most depressing and inept performance I could remember in all my time as a fan, and I had seen plenty of pretty poor games in those years. This was a new kind of bad, a display that made you start to wonder what the point of it all was. Utterly clueless, shapeless, purposeless, hopeless. By Monday, Steve Kember was told that his

time was up, but the truth was that if the players wearing Palace shirts had shown a fraction of the spirit and passion that Kember did as a player, they wouldn't have found themselves in such a parlous state.

With Kit Symons as caretaker manager, the team pulled themselves together and appeared to recover from the trauma of Wigan, but after losing at home to Crewe, a performance that nearly matched that at Wigan for sheer incompetence, it was inevitable that a new manager would replace

IAIN DOWIE

him. In what seemed like the last act of a desperate man, he recalled Julian Gray to the side, who the fans thought they seen the back of, and Palace promptly won the next two games. By now Iain Dowie had been lined up to take over a job that was thought of as a poisoned chalice, with Jordan having earned a reputation as a trigger-happy chairman. Dowie had only spent a few months at Palace as a player back in 1995, but he had made himself popular with his wholehearted efforts, and that was just what was needed to drag Palace out of the bottom three. The Boxing Day defeat at home to Millwall turned out to be the one really bad result for the remainder of the season, and as 2004 got going, the transformation was palpable. Andy Johnson hit a purple patch, Julian

Gray rediscovered his form on the wing, although not enough to get the crowd off his back, and Riihilahti and Hughes both found their best form as Palace stalked their way up the table. Mark Hudson came in to stiffen the defence, and a sequence of five victories, starting with a 5-1 win at Watford, and ending with a 6-3 scoreline against Stoke, pushed them to the fringes of the play-off places. Stoke were at the time the only side with better recent form than Palace, and beating them so comprehensively was evidence of the confidence that Dowie had instilled in his squad, who had looked defeated in every sense just two months earlier.

MIKELE LEIGERTWOOD

The key to Palace's turnaround was the new training regime introduced by Dowie's sidekick, part fitness coach, part motivational evangelist John Harbin, who famously got the players boxing, and based his philosophy on the poem by boxer James Corbett, "One More Round". As well as palpably improving the players' fitness and stamina - even Shipperley started to look slightly trimmer - they started working together as a team with real self-belief. For the first time in years, it was a delight to see Palace making news, and not just in the sports pages. Dowie had coined the word "bouncebackability", which became a minor cultural phenomenon, leading to bouncebackability merchandise, knowing use of the word in other fields, and a petition to have the word included in the Oxford English Dictionary which was ultimately successful. More importantly, it summed up the attitude that was now prevalent throughout the club, on and off the field.

The final two new faces to add to what had become a quite settled side were promising defender Mikele Leigertwood, picked up from the cash-strapped Wimbledon, and keeper Nico Vaesen on loan, Palace's fourth goalie of the season after Matt Clarke, Cedric Berthelin and Thomas Myhre. Still it seemed unlikely that Palace could climb all the way from the bottom three to the top six, and having been offered a week's holiday in Spain at the end of May, I was faced with a big decision knowing that the date clashed with the play-off final. I did all the calculations meticulously, and concluded that it would take a miracle for Palace to be involved, and was pretty happy that I'd made the right decision to book the flights.

A nervy 1-0 win against Walsall in the final home game, with a dodgy penalty decision for Palace, and Johnson's spot kick saved before he followed up to score, meant that a point was needed at Coventry on the final day to seal sixth spot. The game was lost, and with it the play-off place, until West Ham's late equaliser against Wigan which pushed Paul Jewell's side out of the top six and Palace back in, literally at the last minute. If that result had panned out differently, it would still have been an incredible feat for Iain Dowie to have Palace so close, but now there was a real possibility of something even more dramatic. After a couple of frankly turgid years, we now had a huge and meaningful game to look forward to, and the two-legged semi-final against Sunderland didn't disappoint. A goalless first half was followed by a breathless second half, Palace coming from behind to win 3-2, with a late winner from AJ, making it 32 for the season. The second leg three days later was going Sunderland's way when they went 2-0 up by half time, and with 90 minutes gone they still had the lead at 4-3 on aggregate before substitute Darren Powell, who had missed most of the season, headed a goal in injury time to force another 30 minutes. Palace finished with only ten men after a red card for Gray, and finally the game went to penalties. At last we could enjoy the kind of drama that we had been robbed of at Wembley in 1996, and what high drama it was. After Oster hit the post for Sunderland, Palace's Johnson, Freedman, Shipperley and Popovic all scored, leaving Derry to seal it. His shot was saved, and in sudden death Jason McAteer missed to nearly the biggest cheer of the night (in my pub, at least), then Routledge missed, then Jeff Whitley missed, leaving Michael Hughes to step up, cool as you like, and put Palace through to the final. After the tedium of the past two seasons, that moment felt like we had won promotion already, but there was more to do.

With Wembley demolished, the final was to be held in Cardiff, and by all accounts getting there was a complete nightmare, but I had my own travel problems. That was the very day I was flying to Spain for a holiday, and uppermost in my mind were the logistics of getting from the airport to the apartment, and then quickly finding out if there was a bar anywhere showing the game. Dragging a weary family with me, the very first place I tried had a framed aerial photograph of Selhurst Park on the wall, and a passionate Eagle as the owner. Some days things just fall into place, and everything is right with the world, and so it was in Cardiff, as West Ham barely turned up for the game, allowing Neil Shipperley's

tap in to send Palace once again back to the Premiership. By my count this was my seventh promotion as a Palace fan, and by far the most sensational of them all, because after that 5-0 defeat by Wigan in November, it wasn't just unlikely, it was actually impossible.

"Fight one more round. When your feet are so tired that you have to shuffle back to the centre of the ring, fight one more round. When your arms are so tired that you can hardly lift your hands to come on guard, fight one more round. When your nose is bleeding and your eyes are black and you are so tired that you wish that your opponent would crack you one on the jaw and put you to sleep, fight one more round – remembering that the man who always fights one more round is never whipped."

"Gentleman" Jim Corbett

2004-05

"What on earth is Speroni doing trying to dribble the ball out?"

When Division One transmuted into the Premiership in 1992, Palace were briefly founder members, but each attempt to break back in since then had been short-lived. Promotions in '94 and '97, quickly followed by the misery of relegation, had convinced some that perhaps it would be better if we didn't put ourselves through that again. Maybe we should accept our lot as a middling club in the comfort zone of the second tier, by now rebranded as the Championship. I don't hold with that for a moment, and to my mind it's never "a season too soon" to go up. I've grown up with the expectation of a rapid cycle of promotion and relegation, and the few seasons without the promise or threat of either have felt rather pointless. When Arsenal were winning everything under Arsene Wenger, I honestly thought how very dull it must be to follow a team like that, and to expect victory week after week. Any Palace fan will know how far from our own experience that attitude is, and nor do we covet that kind of success. It would be nice to win something now and again, admittedly.

Perhaps Simon Jordan felt a sense of dread at having got Palace to where he wanted, because he started to declare that he was disillusioned with football, and was looking for a way out. He continued that theme wearily for a further six years, and although his stance at the time against the greed of agents seemed admirable, the result was that Palace missed out on signing Tim Cahill, who turned out to be a magnificent player in the Premiership for Everton. Whilst Iain Dowie was committing himself to a further four years, speculation grew about who might relieve Jordan of his tiresome burden, and of course the name of Ron Noades

loomed large, although Jordan's response was: "So long as I've got breath in my body, I won't sell this club back to Ron Noades." A firm moral stance then, against the man who still owned Selhurst Park, and who many blamed for cynically taking Mark Goldberg's imaginary millions. Not such a firm moral stance, though, when it was rumoured that Libya's Colonel Gaddafi was interested: "If it's beneficial to the club, it will be considered. If Gaddafi's money was able to progress Palace and allow them to compete at the top of the tree and be a successful football club, then one would have to take that into consideration." It was nonsense, of course, but Jordan's newly acquired "PR Guru" Max Clifford should have tipped him off that there is such a thing as bad publicity.

GABOR KIRALY

Money was tight, with the windfall of Premiership money barely covering trading losses and liabilities, so Iain Dowie's plans to strengthen to side were hamstrung. Two new goalkeepers arrived, Julian Speroni and Gabor Kiraly, defenders Emmerson Boyce and Fitz Hall, and with Shipperley injured and Julian Gray gone to join Steve Bruce at Birmingham, Palace started the season with a new centre forward, Hungarian Sandor Torghelle, and Finnish winger Joonas Kolkka. None cost very much, and none were a great improvement on the players who had scraped up from Division One. How disheartening it must have been for Derry, Shipperley, Butterfield, Powell and Freedman to find themselves out of the first team, but the reserves did at least have a splendid season. A little more tantalising was the signing of Ivan Kaviedes, an Ecuadorean "icon", we were assured, and then two fringe players on loan from Inter Milan, Nicola Ventola and Gonzalo Sorondo. We still hadn't heard of any of them, and we waited to see whether any of them turned out to be the new Lombardo or the new Padovano.

EMMERSON BOYCE

With points certain to be precious, a draw in the first game at Norwich was welcome, but Palace's entire season turned on one moment in the first home game, against Everton. This was on the face of it a fairly moderate Everton side, who had flirted with relegation the previous season, and it was Palace who looked the better side, taking the lead early on through Mark Hudson's header. At 1-0, the home side continued to dominate and could have scored two or three, but then Julian Speroni, in the Palace goal as first choice ahead of Kiraly, tried to dribble a back pass out of his area, lost the ball to Kevin Campbell, then panicked and brought down the veteran striker for a penalty. As confidence drained from Palace, Everton's grew, and a game that Palace

were looking like winning slipped away from them, with Marcus Bent's goal for 3-1 being particularly galling. Bent had been popular during his time at Palace, but had been inexplicably neglected by Terry Venable before leaving for Port Vale, and in a way it was gratifying, if painful, to see how far he had come since then. Speroni's confidence was shot to pieces after that howler, and soon Kiraly came into the team, staying put for nearly three years.

Tommy Black was another player who found himself side-lined, and at one point both and he and Dougie Freedman were about to sign for Leeds, until Freedman declared that he wanted to stay and fight for his place in the team, and take his number of goals past 100. Sandor Torghelle quickly dropped out of the reckoning up front, and one would have expected Freedman to renew his partnership with AJ, which had looked exceptional at times, but instead Iain Dowie decided to switch to a formation with five in midfield and Johnson on his own up front. This did have an effect in the short term, with Johnson continuing to score freely, but it meant that Palace were becoming a little one dimensional, with no Plan B. However, when Arsenal came to Selhurst Park at the beginning of November, things seemed to be falling into place, and Aki Riihilahti rounded off a barnstorming performance with the equaliser in a game that Palace deserved to win.

That game was to be the highlight of the first half of the season, though, and Palace failed to win in the course of the next ten games, finding themselves in the bottom three by Christmas. Routledge had started to alienate himself from the fans by making it clear that he wanted a move to a bigger club, despite growing up at Palace; Kaviedes had disappeared having "failed to settle", and Greek international Vassilis Lakis had taken over from Kolkka on the left, but it felt as if Dowie was running out of ideas. Johnson continued to score regularly, including a spell of nine goals in as many games, and was finally selected to play out of position on the right wing for England, but if he wasn't scoring nobody else was. Freedman's return to the team coincided with a surprising 3-0 victory over Spurs, but on the whole Dowie's team selection became erratic, Popovic dropped from the side, young Tom Soares being preferred to Ben Watson, and Wayne Andrews on the bench emphasising the thinness of Palace's squad. For a team in trouble, to let the January transfer window pass by without adding to the squad was distressing and, sure enough, Palace were by now firmly entrenched in the bottom four.

SANDOR TORGHELLE

Palace's famed bouncebackability made an appearance with a satisfying 1-0 victory over Liverpool, and the battling spirit shown by players like Hughes and Riihilahti announced that once again Palace would respond to Dowie's urgings to fight one more round. Draws against Newcastle and Southampton, both attritional slugging matches, set up the final day of the season, a game at Charlton which Palace needed to win to stay up. That penultimate game against the Saints would turn out to be Sorondo's last for Palace as he was sent off after a punch up with Peter Crouch, with Graham le Saux provoking a mass brawl, and featured a rare appearance for Nicola Ventola as substitute. This was only Ventola's third appearance all season, and the tidy goal that he scored turned out to be the only goal of the entire campaign for a striker other than AJ. It appeared to have won a reprieve for Palace, but Southampton equalised in injury time, keeping their own hopes alive, and on the last day relegation came down to any three out of four.

JOONAS KOLKKA

Needing three points against Charlton at the Valley, Iain Dowie picked Ben Watson ahead of Riihilahti, and restored Butterfield to the defence, but in a surprisingly open game, Palace found themselves a goal behind at half time. Cometh the hour, cometh the Doug, and as soon as Freedman came off the bench the game swung Palace's way. Freedman scored a beautifully judged chip, then won a penalty, put away by Johnson, to surely save his team from relegation once again. Watching from distance on the big screen at Selhurst Park, I couldn't see precisely what was going on, although what I could make out seemed to suggest safety with just eight minutes to go, before a poorly defended free kick into the box gave Charlton their second, and sent Palace out of the Premiership yet again, to the glee of the locals.

This relegation felt different somehow to the others. Palace certainly weren't a shambles, like in 1998, nor could they point to terrible bad luck, as in 1995. Instead, we had to accept that we were just that little bit off being good enough, and could just as well have finished mid-table as bottom, but simply hadn't strengthened the squad sufficiently to bridge the gap between the top two divisions. Ventola might have been the striker we needed, but he was injured for most of his time at the club, and despite efforts to sign Tim Cahill and Dean Ashton - either of whom could well have kept Palace up - those deals came to nothing. Iain Dowie had to struggle on with what he had, and the team that finished the season wasn't noticeably better than the one that had won promotion at Cardiff a year earlier.

2005-06

"100 years of Passion and Pride"

So went the strapline for Palace's centenary year, and it was a good season to reflect on what that meant, to us as fans, and to players. As footballers have become increasingly mercenary, so the laughable hypocrisy of kissing the shirt to curry favour has become more and more prevalent, and increasingly nauseating. Mercifully, we haven't seen too much of it at Selhurst Park, although a few instances stand out, and you want to believe that players like Lombardo share your undying love for the club they probably hadn't heard of until a few months ago. When Sasa Curcic declared: "I will only leave this club if they carry me out in a dead box," it gave us something to cling on to in that bleak season. There are a few players, though, who renew your faith that there is still the concept of loyalty, and a genuine bond with the fans, and despite relegation for Palace there was a true sense of unity. I believed Aki Riihilahti when he wrote, just the day after relegation against Charlton: "I'd have done anything for us to stay up. It is painful and I've been crying a lot since yesterday. I put everything into it and still it wasn't enough." I believed him every time he celebrated a goal; when he kissed the badge with a furious defiance as relegation drew inexorably closer, he meant it, and had earned the right to display his passion. Dougie Freedman had showed us what Crystal Palace meant to him when he refused to leave, and pledged to fight for his place in the team, despite being ill-used by both Trevor Francis and Iain Dowie.

Andy Johnson, though, had shown himself to be a class act in the Premiership, was in the England squad, and had done his level best for Palace, so after he put in a transfer request, it was only a question of which team could afford him. However it was that Dowie and Simon Jordan eventually persuaded him to stay, whilst he was being courted by Spurs and Everton during the summer, it was a massive boost to the fans, and a guarantee, surely, of another promotion season ahead. Gabor Kiraly had also impressed a number of clubs, but chose to stay, although the foreign legion of Lakis, Sorondo, Ventola and Torghelle all sloped

GONZALO SORONDO

off, to be followed soon after by Joonas Kolkka. Apart from Sorondo, none left a huge gap, but the most significant departure was that of Wayne Routledge, who had outgrown the club who had looked after him as a boy, given him his debut aged 16, and turned him into a Premiership footballer, electing instead to sign for Spurs reserves. His direct replacement was Jobi McAnuff, a proper winger who had grown up at Wimbledon with Mikele Leigertwood, and who had developed into a good Championship player with Cardiff. Iain Dowie replaced Sorondo with Darren Ward from Millwall, and with the need still for an old fashioned centre forward in his own image, rescued Jon Macken from Manchester City, where he had slowly declined after they had paid £5.5million for him a couple of years earlier.

Another club in the market for Andy Johnson was Birmingham, who had realised what an error they had made in letting him go as part of the Clinton Morrison deal, and their chairman David Gold continued his spat with Jordan when he reiterated the idea that AJ needed to be playing in the Premiership to keep his England place. Morrison was by now out of favour with Steve Bruce at Birmingham, and appeared to be heading to Norwich until Palace came up with the wonderful idea of bringing him back to play alongside Johnson. Morrison declared himself Palace through and through, and made the move. Never go back, they say. It worked for Dougie Freedman when he came home to Selhurst Park, but not for David Hopkin, who returned as a shadow of the player he had been. Steve Kember had two successful

DARREN WARD

spells to bookmark his career, and later on Peter Nicholas, Andy Gray and Neil Shipperley were all welcomed back, but what would we be getting with Clinton Morrison? A more mature and thoughtful player, desperate to give his all for club who nurtured him, or someone disenchanted by slipping down the hierarchy at Birmingham?

Macken was already labouring up front against Stoke when Clinton came on as substitute for his first game back, and combined with AJ for Johnson's second goal of the game, and naturally much badge-kissing followed. In the next game, he started up front alongside AJ, and they both scored, and the same happened in the game after that. This was looking a masterstroke by Dowie, and Macken soon found himself struggling to get in the team, but when Johnson faced several weeks out with a knee injury, we were treated once again to the double act of Freedman and Morrison from four years earlier. For a spell the two of them clicked and Freedman was back to his best, scoring six goals in five games, moving Palace towards the top end of the table, and taking in yet another League Cup tie against Liverpool. The idea of beating Liverpool in a knockout game was by now becoming commonplace, and goals from Marco Reich and Freedman won the game for Palace, although the outstanding player on the night was the forgotten man, Julian Speroni, who had kept clean sheets in the two previous rounds, with Kiraly rested, and showed what a spectacular shot stopper he could be. Freedman's 100th goal finally came in the 3-2 victory at Brighton, avenging their 1-0 win at Selhurst Park just a month earlier, and although Palace were a little below where they had expected to be approaching Christmas, an unprecedented winning streak of four wins in eight days over the holidays put them back in the running for the play-offs.

It already seemed, though, that Steve Coppell's Reading and Sheffield United were running away with the automatic promotion places, so the season became a steady jog to stay in the top six for several teams, rather than a sprint to the finish. The latter part of the season was characterised by the good form of McAnuff, both wide and in front of goal, the indifferent form of Morrison, and the welcome return of Aki Riihilahti from injury. Some questioned whether Aki would win back his place with Soares and Watson preferred, alongside the evergreen Michael Hughes, but in his few remaining appearances he reminded everyone what a valuable all-round asset he was, getting forward to score a couple despite his reputation as a destroyer. By the time the home game with Watford came around, the top of the table had more or less sorted itself out and both sides were already thinking ahead half a dozen games to the play-offs. Palace ran out pretty comfortable 3-1 winners, whilst Dowie experimented in a few positions; Popovic made a rare start in defence, and Riihilahti dropped to the bench. We didn't realise at the time, but this was to be the last time that Aki pulled on a Palace shirt, and he didn't even get on the pitch. The following few games saw starts for Reich, Macken and Butterfield, who had all become fringe players, but none of made the cut for the vital first leg of the play-off semi-final, where Palace were to face Watford once again.

JULIAN SPERONI

Here we were again, not going up as champions, as Simon Jordan had confidently promised, but scraping through to fight one more round, which looked a formality against a Watford team that had looked anything but stiff opposition a few weeks earlier. The question was whether we would prefer Preston or Leeds in the final, but on the day Palace showed no pride, no desire, and capitulated 3-0, which was almost embarrassing. A 0-0 draw at Vicarage Road was remarkable only for a huge punch-up after Fitz Hall tried to wrestle the ball from Watford's time-wasting manager, but that was more passion than anyone in the team had shown all season, a season that ended in disappointment and a little sadness, as it was to be the last we would see not only of Iain Dowie's victory punch to the Holmesdale end, but of Andy Johnson's burger-munching goal celebration, and of the great Aki Riihilahti.

"I pictured myself in Cardiff, on the podium celebrating in the sea of red and blue another promotion for the club I've been privileged to play for over five years. In that moment of complete fulfilment I could have even sang along my tone deaf version of 'Glad all over'. Victorious moment, a mutual thank you – have a good summer! That would have been my perfect ending for this season. Instead my great years in Crystal Palace might have ended to a disappointing result, on a grey evening sitting behind the dugout at Vicarage Road kicking a seat in front in despair. Small injuries and a failed promotion campaign leaves a bitter taste to what has been done over the years. You don't want to be remembered as bit of a sick note after you've played 180 games for the club. Or that you didn't achieve the widely expected promotion after the club was almost relegated from the same league when you joined. In the history of sports, though, you are always as good as your last game."

Aki Riihilahti, 16 May 2006

"Peter Taylor will get Palace playing exciting, attacking football in his own image..."

Only two people really know what was said in a long and difficult telephone conversation between Simon Jordan and Iain Dowie, and as they have since settled out of court, it will stay that way. The outcome was that less than a fortnight after the 2005-06 season ended, the news broke that Dowie was leaving Crystal Palace "by mutual consent". In Simon Jordan's version, he suggested that Andy Johnson, Fitz Hall, Ben Watson and Tom Soares should be sold. Dowie disagreed. Jordan suggested sitting down and watching a video of the Watford game together "so that I could better understand his viewpoint and how he saw the game." Dowie's response, according to Jordan, was "under no circumstances am I going to watch matches with you, if you want to manage, do your coaching badges." Crucially, again according to Jordan's version, Dowie said that he wanted to leave to be nearer his family, who lived in Bolton, and as a result Jordan waived a contracted £1 million compensation payment. One thing the two men did agree on, when both were cross-examined in court, was that each had grown to dislike the other quite some time ago, and both knew it.

The press conference that confirmed Dowie's departure had been preceded by a rumour that Dowie was going to take over at Charlton, who had just removed their highly successful manager Alan Curbishley, but according to Jordan, he had assurances from Dowie that he wouldn't be going to the Valley under any circumstances. Within a week, Charlton confirmed that Dowie was to take the manager's job, but Jordan had a coup lined up for their press conference, trying to get a writ served on Dowie, accusing him of misrepresentation, and making sure that the camera crews present were tipped off. This was characteristic of Jordan's showboating style, and whatever the truth of the matter, at the time I knew whose word I would be inclined to trust out of the two of them. I thought that Dowie had done wonders at Palace, and that Jordan should have done all he could to keep him there, but the relationship had clearly run its course.

After a very public bidding war involving Bolton and Wigan, Andy Johnson wisely chose to move to Everton, and Palace happily pocketed £8.6million, easily the most ever received for a Palace player. Unusually for a player so crucial to their team, there was nothing but good will from the fans as AJ left, as not only was it obvious that he could have gone much sooner, but everyone recognised his complete commitment to Palace's cause whenever he pulled on the shirt, unlike other recent departees such as Julian Gray and Wayne Routledge. Palace also got decent fees from Wigan for Fitz Hall and Emmerson Boyce, both of whom had done enough during Palace's Premiership season to earn a move to another side likely to struggle at the top level, but Sheffield United signed Mikele Leigertwood on the cheap, meaning that three of Palace's most able defenders had gone within weeks of each other.

The curious thing about Jordan's latest quest for a new manager was that he was assisted by Bob Dowie, brother of Iain, who had remained in his rather mysterious role of Director of Football. Among candidates considered were Luton's Mike Newell, and remarkably - again - Graeme Souness, but in luring Peter Taylor from Hull, Jordan divided opinion like never before. There was no question that Taylor had been a fabulous player for Palace under Malcolm Allison, and had been instrumental in getting Palace to their first ever FA Cup semi-final in 1976. He was immensely popular, a true winger who could get past players and put in killer crosses from either side, and he did a mean Norman Wisdom impression to boot. As a manager, though, the jury was still out. Taylor had done well at Gillingham, Brighton and Hull, earning promotion from the lower leagues with each. He also had a good reputation for his work with the England under-21s, even taking charge of the full England team as caretaker manager for one game. Most people, though, remembered that he had failed at Leicester City, and he was destined

PETER TAYLOR

to forever be associated with his star signing, the woeful Ade Akinbiyi. There were those who had wanted Taylor as manager for years, hoping that he would bring some of the flamboyance he showed as a player, and perhaps some of the glamour of the Allison years, when Palace plummeted from the first to the third division, but the crowds kept coming. Others were worried that, if and when he fell out with Jordan and was fired, it would overshadow the memories of those happier times. Sometimes you just don't want to know that your heroes are fallible human beings like you, but there it was, and perhaps Peter Taylor had found his destiny, to guide the Eagles to glory and become a legend.

With what should have been a considerable sum of money to spend, he set about bringing in new faces, and the hope was that he would already have a list of promising young talent in his back pocket as a result of his England job and could attract them to Palace to join the likes of Watson, Soares and Borrowdale. We could be looking at something like Venables' young guns of 1979 here. Leon Cort - 14 caps for England under-21s - came from Hull, and looked a good centre back, perhaps a fair replacement for Fitz Hall. Next in was the young goalkeeper Scott Flinders from Barnsley, who had played for the England under-20s. Here we go, who's next? Charlie Sheringham, 18-year-old son of England's Teddy Sheringham. Looking good. James Scowcroft, aged 30? Well, maybe he can do a job up front. Carl Fletcher, a bit of Premiership experience with West Ham,

CARL FLETCHER

OK, I suppose. Matt Lawrence... didn't he play alongside Darren Ward when Millwall got to the FA Cup final a couple of years back, but isn't he knocking on a bit? And Mark Kennedy... he used to be quite good, I seem to recall.

In all honesty, it was beginning to look like Peter Taylor was putting together a side to stay in the Championship rather than take it by storm, but the first three games confounded that theory. Three straight wins sent Palace to the summit; Scowcroft and Cort both got goals and looked good, Mark Kennedy could hit a dead ball better than the consistently disappointing Ben Watson, and Morrison and Freedman both got off the mark for the season. However, it was soon apparent that Taylor really didn't rate one of the great strike partnerships in Palace history, and with Jon Macken ditched, Torghelle finally gone, and not even Wayne Andrews on the bench to come on and run around a bit, the search was on for a big-name, big-money striker. David Nugent, Izale Mcleod and Freddy Eastwood were

MATT LAWRENCE

all on the radar, but eventually the transfer window closed with the big news that Shefki Kuqi had been signed for £2.5million, and the rather smaller news of Peter Taylor's son-in-law Stuart Green arriving from Hull. Kuqi had been a fine player at Ipswich, taking the eye with his goal celebration which involved diving through the air to land outstretched on his belly, and had spent time in the Premiership at Blackburn, although with less impact. Nevertheless, here was a seasoned international, a team mate of Aki Riihilahti in the Finland side, and someone who had a proven record in the Championship. It seemed a lot of money, but we had got over £8 million for AJ, after all.

It didn't take long for Palace's early season sparkle to die away, just as it didn't take long for everyone to realise that Kuqi was mostly a waste of a perfectly good XXL shirt, but there was a seemingly happy distraction when Simon Jordan smugly announced that he had secretly bought the freehold of Selhurst Park from Ron Noades, under the guise of another company: "I bought Selhurst Park through a structure that was set up over the last two weeks and I'm not so sure that Ron is aware of who he has sold it to, but he's sold it to me." This sounded like wonderful news, as it meant that Palace could now get on with developing the ground in the way they wanted, or at the very least fixing the toilets. Whatever the voices inside Jordan's head were telling him, this turned out not to be true.

By the end of October, and after an appalling run of results, the calls for Peter Taylor to be sacked were ringing out loud and clear, but the first to walk the plank was Bob Dowie, whose role and influence over the manager was unclear from the start. There was much speculation about the nature of the underlying problems, but problems there most certainly were. Taylor had no idea of his best side, swapping Granville and Borrowdale, Ward and Hudson, Fletcher and Michael Hughes, and even Marco Reich got a bit of a look in, but most strangely, he dropped Kiraly, first of all trying Scott Flinders, then the on-loan Iain Turner, with all the while Julian Speroni sitting idly on the bench. It could have been curtains for the manager after Simon Jordan gave him his own personal vote of confidence, but from nowhere results started to pick up, and Kuqi and Freedman briefly started to look like a useful strike partnership, notably in the 3-0 home win over QPR, which bought Taylor some time, perhaps enough time to make some meaningful signings in the January transfer window.

Taylor had fallen out with so many players at various times- Morrison, McAnuff, Ward, Kiraly, Morrison and Hughes amongst them - and so many had lost their form, that radical changes were needed, but the only new faces were Paul Ifill and Dave Martin, wingers both. Ifill was another Millwall old boy who had lost his way a bit at Sheffield United under Neil Warnock, and Martin was catching the eye at non-league Dartford, but in reality it wasn't wingers we needed, and although Ifill made a decent start, helping Palace to a seven-game unbeaten run, neither signing was what was needed to kick start the season.

SHEFKI KUQI

Ultimately, it was a season that had promised little, and delivered less. As springtime approached, and despite a general improvement in performances, it was increasingly unlikely that the last couple of months would offer anything other than paddling in mid-table, and so it proved, but there were just enough green shoots for Taylor to be given more time, with promise of a better season to come. Overall, though, of Peter Taylor's signings, Cort had been the best and Fletcher had worked as hard as he could, but he had completely failed to build what could really be called a team. The fans hadn't enjoyed the manager's largely negative approach, surely a symptom of

Taylor's fear of the sack more than of his natural instincts, and there had been little to get hot under the collar about. Some players underachieved, notably Watson and Soares, and some just weren't good enough. Was Taylor a bad manager, were they bad players, or was it just bad luck? Honestly, a bit of all three, but this was a season to be forgotten, reminiscent of the time under Trevor Francis, and in every sense the club had gone backwards.

"If we can build a team around young Bostock, we can really go places..."

The only thing less likely than Peter Taylor still being in charge would be Jamie Scowcroft scoring a hat-trick, but the first game of the season, away to Southampton, saw both. It was to be the pinnacle of Taylor's Palace career as a manager, and perhaps even Scowcroft's, whose goals the previous season had been carefully rationed. Perhaps Simon Jordan was a changed man, and had been stung by criticism that he was too quick to fire managers, but there had been enough improvement, albeit from a very low starting point, for him to have faith that Peter Taylor was starting to get things right. There had been a big clear out of players during the summer, with Watford paying good money for Jobi McAnuff, and Darren Ward, Gary Borrowdale and Danny Granville all moving on, as well as Gabor Kiraly, Michael Hughes and Tommy Black. That's quite a few players to replace, but with nobody willing to take Kuqi off his hands, Jordan was finding cash flow increasingly problematic, and apart from Portuguese defender Jose Fonte, the pre-season spend was restricted to left back Tony Craig, yet another ordinary Millwall player, and left winger Jeff Hughes from Lincoln City. Remember them?

Following the fine win at Southampton, Palace were dumped out of the League Cup on penalties by Bristol Rovers, with Freedman and Kuqi both missing from the spot. Palace then scraped a point at home against Leicester through Morrison's goal in injury time, moving him on to 99 goals for the club. Three defeats later, though, and there were already strong rumours that Peter Taylor was going to be replaced as manager by Neil Warnock, which Simon Jordan denied. Taylor had lost patience with Kuqi, who went to Fulham on loan, and

still couldn't see that Dougie Freedman was his only hope of salvation, so he went into the loan market and signed up Paul Dickov and Besian Idrizaj. The young Dickov had been one of the scorers in Arsenal's 3-0 victory that sent Palace out of the Premiership under Steve Coppell, and had gone on to earn a reputation as a combative forward for a number of clubs, while Idrizaj was a promising young Austrian striker on Liverpool's books, and came to Selhurst Park on a season-long loan. Neither made much impact, neither scored, and neither was able to save the manager's bacon.

NEIL WARNOCK

Quite why it took Simon Jordan so long to put Peter Taylor out of our misery, I'm not sure, but the reaction to the news could only ever be a shrug, a tilt of the head and a few kind words: "it's for the best." Coppell, Smith, Bruce, Kember, Francis, Dowie, Taylor, all managers since Jordan's takeover in 2000, all sacked by Jordan, apart from Sir Steve, who sacked himself, yet for some reason Neil Warnock wanted the job. Frequently described as the Marmite manager - you either love him or hate him - more often you either hate him because he's the opposition's manager, or hate him despite him being yours. Without question, Warnock knew the business of managing struggling football teams inside out, and it came as no surprise to find that a man so wilfully controversial and outspoken counted Simon Jordan as a close personal friend. Underneath it all, Warnock's penchant for winding up fans, players and officials was sharply calculating, but he loved nothing more than upsetting people, which at times was hilarious, at other times tedious. Most recently, he had been in charge of a Sheffield United side relegated from the Premiership on the last day, and felt the injustice of West Ham's survival at their expense very deeply after they were fined for playing Carlos Tevez in breach of regulations but not deducted any points.

After the torpor of Peter Taylor's reign, it didn't really matter what Palace fans thought of Warnock personally, because one way or another things might get interesting at last. It was early enough in the season for the fans to put up with the inevitable period of transition, and indeed Warnock's first win didn't come for seven games, but by then he had started to rip the squad apart and rebuild it in his own image. Out went some of the players perceived as Taylor's men, including Leon Cort, Stuart Green and Mark Kennedy, as well as the new signings Tony Craig and Jeff Hughes, and in came Clint Hill at left back, and somewhat surprisingly, Shaun Derry, who hadn't been a great favourite in his precious spell. The contrast between Leon Cort, considered "too nice" by Warnock, and without enough scars on his face, and the uncompromising defender Hill, not averse to receiving or dishing out a few scars, was an indication of Warnock's determination to add some grit, and the return of Derry was further confirmation of what we could look forward to. From November through to the middle of January, Warnock galvanised his team to such an extent that they went unbeaten for fifteen games, and stormed up the table and into the top six. The transformation

in some of the players was remarkable. Clinton Morrison, who had generally been moping around under Taylor, found his scoring form again, and Jamie Scowcroft started to look a good foil for Clinton, as well as popping in a few himself, with a memorable long-range strike at Wolves. Danny Butterfield returned to the side, with Matt Lawrence joining Hudson in the centre of defence, and Speroni's form in goal ensured that Kiraly wasn't missed.

CLINT HILL

More surprising was that, with Warnock's reputation for strong, battling teams, he nevertheless started to experiment with some of the more promising young players who strangely hadn't got a look in under Taylor. Victor Moses had been spoken of as a future star for a while, and Warnock eased him into the side gently, while Sean Scannell made a big impact with his pace and had a good run in the side. Young Lee Hills was given his debut and showed great promise, but for a while all the talk was of John Bostock, also given his debut by Neil Warnock, aged just fifteen. Bostock had been at the club since the age of seven, and had been spoken of as a real prodigy, a future star of English football, destined to captain his country one day. Best of all, his family were true Palace fans, and he intended staying at Palace despite interest already from Arsenal, Chelsea, even

Barcelona. He showed tantalising glimpses of his talent in his few cameo appearances, and then he was put away for the winter, until he could sign a professional contract on his sixteenth birthday. When he then signed for Spurs reserves, Jordan was livid with Bostock's stepfather, accusing him of lying to him about wanting to stay, and with the Football League tribunal who set the fee at a paltry £700,000: "We had a £900,000 offer from Chelsea when he was 14 which we turned down. It's beyond me and it makes me question why I bother with football. I have an academy who have produced a world-class footballer for someone else and got paid two-and-sixpence for it. We weren't unrealistic - we didn't try to be clever and put a value of £5million on the player. We simply said this is what the player is worth, these are the reasons why he is worth it and all we wanted was a fair and equitable outcome." You had to say, whatever you thought of Jordan's righteous indignation in other areas, that he had a pretty fair point here, and he certainly convinced the Palace faithful that their club had been badly wronged.

Shaun Derry was a revelation under Warnock, twice the player he had been in his first spell at Palace, and his loan deal was made permanent, as was Clint Hill's, and midfielder Neil Danns was signed from Birmingham, although he barely played for another year. With Scowcroft and Morrison hitting a barren patch, to halt the slide down the table Warnock tried a curious experiment, bringing Shefki Kuqi back into the team as a lone striker. The experiment only lasted a couple of games and once again the crowd was on his back to such an extent that when he was rightfully substituted in a home game against Wolves, the fans showed their unanimous delight at him leaving the pitch. We don't have a satisfactory name for the gesture that Kuqi

responded with, but in French it is known as the "bras d'honneur", in Spanish as "el corte de manga", and in any language the meaning is clear: "up yours!" Perhaps we should call it the Kuqi in English. Neil Warnock acted swiftly to fine Kuqi and put him on the transfer list, and we were sure that was the last we had seen of the Flying Finn. It turned out that we were wrong, but we were shortly to see the last of Dougie Freedman in a Palace shirt. Freedman had only started three games under Warnock (yet another manager with a blind spot for the most gifted footballer at the club), and reluctantly agreed to go on loan to Leeds for the remainder of the season, where he quickly showed his quality and helped them into the League One play-offs.

SEAN SCANNELL

With Victor Moses and Sean Scannell now becoming established in the side, Warnock continued to do what he does best. He kept Palace in contention for the play-off places, finally ensuring their involvement after a 5-0 rout of Burnley on the final day, with the on-loan Scott Sinclair looking like the player who might give Palace the edge in the scrap for promotion. Their semi-final opponents, Bristol City, had been in the top six all season and in the top two for a while, but looked vulnerable to a Palace side on a late run into the play-offs, much as we had witnessed in Iain Dowie's first season.

City always had the edge in the first leg at Selhurst Park and it looked for a while as if Dele Adebola might be the man to win it for the visitors, five years after he had left Palace, but it was a superb long range goal from David Noble that gave City a 2-1 lead to defend at Bristol three days later. Palace didn't make it easy, and took the lead with a Ben Watson header, and then won a penalty which would have put them ahead on aggregate. Everything was set up for Ben Watson, who had grown into a crucial part of Warnock's team, to complete the job, but his shot hit the post and the game swung City's way, winning 2-1 after extra time. It should have felt like a massive let-down, but the atmosphere at Bristol that evening wasn't at all downbeat. Palace had lost fair and square, but hadn't really expected to be contesting the play-offs after the way the season started, and it seemed like an awful long time since we'd had such enjoyable, competitive games with something at stake. Neil Warnock may be a bastard, but he was our bastard, and with a full season next year he would surely get Palace back into the Premiership.

"Ashley-Paul is goin fulham on Monday. If I pull dis off im on dis ting!!!"

Ashley-Paul Robinson was another promising academy player who had made a few substitute appearances towards the end of Neil Warnock's first season, and had looked a fast, skilful winger, if a little tubby. As a result he had been offered a contract at Palace, but he chose to let the world know that he belonged in the Premiership by announcing a trial at Fulham on his Facebook page, thus ending his Palace career with a few misjudged keystrokes, and clearing his path to the lower reaches of non-league football. As fast as Palace's

PADDY McCARTHY

youth system could produce players fit for first team action, it seemed, they had a battle on their hands to keep them at the club, John Bostock being the most notorious instance. Now Ben Watson wanted a move, and Victor Moses was being courted by Premiership teams, as were Tom Soares and Sean Scannell. Morrison had also rejected a new contract and moved to Coventry, and Dougie Freedman eventually signed for Southend after being told that he wasn't in Warnock's plans for the coming season. Mark Hudson joined Charlton, and even Simon Jordan renewed his efforts to sell the club and get as far away from football as possible.

So without Morrison, Freedman, and probably Watson, and with Scowcroft and Ifill transfer-listed, what were the manager's grand plans to improve on the previous year? Attacking midfielder Nick Carle in for Watson to start with, the Australian international having impressed for Bristol City in the play-off games against Palace. Centre back Paddy McCarthy came from Charlton, which seemed to be a straightforward like-for-like swap, but with Kuqi still festering while waiting for someone else to take on his considerable wage bill, extra manpower was needed up front and the only forwards coming in were Luton's Calvin Andrew and non-league player Simon Thomas.

The opening game, a 0-0 draw with Watford, was dull affair, as was a 2-1 defeat of Hereford in the League Cup, which featured two other new signings in John Oster and Leandre Griffit. Those two drab performances set the tone for the early part of the season, with all eyes on the transfer window. Stoke City paid a lot of money for Tom Soares, but there were no moves for Moses, Scannell or Watson, and Palace eventually got the centre forward that was so desperately needed to get the season going, Ipswich's Alan Lee. Lee was injured almost immediately, but the season did appear to be improving when Ben Watson returned to the fold against Swansea and played a blinder, scoring directly from a free kick which he had intended as a cross. With Lee absent, Neil Warnock moved quickly to loan another striker, Craig Beattie from West Bromwich Albion, who were by now in the Premiership. Beattie made a huge difference and although he wasn't prolific in front of goal he contributed a lot to an improvement in form that saw Palace move almost unnoticed into the top six by Christmas. Sadly, Beattie was needed back at West Brom, but while he had been there Warnock had unexpectedly given another chance to Kuqi, which smacked of desperation. However, Kuqi confounded everyone by giving total commitment on the pitch, scoring a few excellent goals, and winning over the very fans who he had despised a year earlier. He still wasn't all that good, in truth, but was worth his place on effort alone, and for his continuing comedy value.

One young player about to make his mark was Nathaniel Clyne, who had gone into the first team almost unheralded, but who immediately looked the business - shades of what we saw of Ashley Cole during his time on loan - but Ben Watson was finally on his way, to Wigan, now managed by Jordan's old adversary Steve Bruce. Watson's departure, followed closely by McCarthy's absence with a dislocated shoulder, signalled a sharp downturn in results, and with no points in January, and only four in February, hopes of promotion started to recede. Alan Lee came into the team, lumbered about to little effect before going out on loan

ALAN LEE

to Norwich, Oster's early promise tailed off, and Carle and Ifill continued to be huge disappointments. An indication of the financial storm clouds gathering was the decision to let Danny Butterfield go on loan to Charlton, so that Palace could afford

to bring in striker Anthony Stokes until the end of the season. It was evident from the lack of new signings, apart from centre back Claude Davis, that money was a big issue despite the earlier sales of Soares and Watson, and the season proved yet again to be a damp squib, made all the harder to accept after flirtation with the play-offs a year earlier. Palace under Neil Warnock had gone back to more or less the mediocre state he had found them in, and it was hard to see a way forward if funds really were that scarce.

By far the best thing about this forgettable season was the playing strip, with Palace reverting to the diagonal red and blue sash for the first time at home since 1986. First introduced in 1976, the sash was evocative of the Malcolm Allison era, of Venables' later "Team of the Eighties", and of the bleaker years under Dario Gradi, Alan Mullery and, more happily Steve Coppell. Ian Walsh and Dave Swindlehurst scored in the sash when they beat Burnley for promotion in 1979, Jim Cannon when he scored to put the Eagles top of Division One the following season, and Ian Wright made his debut and scored his first Palace goals wearing the sash. It wasn't just nostalgia on the part of us old geezers, though, as the sash had been voted for by the fans who on the whole loved it and wanted to keep it. After a single season, though, commercial considerations and a complete disregard for the views of the fans meant that it was due to be ditched in favour of a generic Red and Blue striped design supplied off the peg by Nike. The Croydon Advertiser gave voice to some of the fans who were upset by this, and Simon Jordan's petty reaction was to ban the Advertiser from the ground, demonstrating to one and all just how much he had lost the plot.

The season ended as it had begun, with a goalless draw, at home to Sheffield United during which Jose Fonte's younger brother Rui, on loan from Arsenal, came on as a substitute. As the Blades still had a shot at automatic promotion, it was good game in front of a large crowd, but Fonte's involvement after his loan period had ended meant that Palace were later deducted one point, although it made no difference to the final position of fifteenth in the table. There had been a few good things to reflect on: the superb form in goal of Julian Speroni, fast becoming a cult figure, the development of Moses, Scannell and Clyne, and Neil

CLAUDE DAVIS

Danns starting to look a very good player after a year out injured, but too many players had flopped for the season to be counted as anything but a let-down. In fact Palace were so firmly in fifteenth, their rightful position after a poor season, that had they been awarded ten extra points, or deducted ten points, they still would have been solidly embedded in the hinterland of the Championship.

"Going down? Are we f***, Minus ten, and we're staying up!"

Neil Warnock clearly felt that he had unfinished business, with the expectation that he would stay at Palace until Simon Jordan had found a buyer, and then retire to the West Country. The turnover of players continued, but Alan Lee remained, Kuqi having finally left, and the ageing striker Stern John was signed for a year along with West Ham's young star Freddie Sears,

STERN JOHN

on loan. That was the strike partnership that started the season against Plymouth, with unknown French youngster Alassane N'Diaye in midfield, Warnock having already hyped him as the new Patrick Viera. On the bench was another new signing, Darren Ambrose, who had joined from Charlton, and who had helped them to relegation along with Mark Hudson and Danny Butterfield. Ambrose had shone as a young player at Ipswich, but had never quite made it in the Premiership with Newcastle, and appeared to have a similar career trajectory to Mark Kennedy, whose time at Palace had been inauspicious.

Stern John's first game ended in him being stretchered off with a dislocated elbow, but Alan Lee came on from the bench, scored a goal, and kept his place for most of the season, slowly winning the fans round as he battled away manfully. A midweek cup tie against Torquay saw Ambrose score his first two goals for Palace, and he retained his place the following Saturday for the trip to old adversaries Bristol City. Freddie Sears got round the back of the defence, and poked the ball past the goalkeeper for his first goal for Palace. Not the cleanest strike, admittedly, but they all count, and Sears lapped up the congratulations as the City defenders walked disconsolately away ready for the restart. The referee, though, and his assistant, were the only two people who didn't spot that the ball had bounced out after hitting the horizontal support at the back of the net, and awarded a goal kick. The disgrace of it was not that the two officials made such a howler, but that the Bristol City players didn't put them straight. The use of the word "cheat" by Jordan and Warnock upset the City manager Gary Johnson, but sometimes that can be quite an apt word.

DARREN AMBROSE

The revelation of the season turned out to be Darren Ambrose, whose quality on the ball and passing ability was better than anything we had seen for a while, and Danns started to come into his own, looking far more effective than either Carle or Oster had been. But the start of the season was overshadowed by a transfer embargo placed on Palace by the Football League over unpaid bonuses and signing-on fees to ex-players, and one started to understand why players such as Ifill, Scowcroft and Oster had appeared disgruntled. Simon Jordan managed to pay off whatever was owed to get the embargo lifted, but then another followed, this time due to money owed to Ipswich for Alan Lee. "I'm aware of the situation and we will get around it," said Jordan...

We blinked, and it was as if the past ten years hadn't happened. Perhaps Marx got it the wrong way round when he observed that history repeats itself, first as tragedy, then as farce. Even the most earnest fan would concede that the Goldberg era and ensuing administration was pure farce, never more so than when the legendary Attilio Lombardo was placed in charge of team affairs with so little grasp of English that Tomas Brolin was kept on to act as interpreter (and even got to squeeze into a shirt and play). As bleak as the outcome was, there was nevertheless a feeling that each week would bring some new comic twist to the story, and the heroics of Steve Coppell in securing safety the following season with the most threadbare of squads ensured a happy ending. Indeed, it was during these dark days that we saw some of the great moments in Palace history, Dougie Freedman sealing his legendary status at Stockport, and the formation of the Trust showing the blitz spirit among the fans.

The difference this time, as Simon Jordan steered the club towards the rocks, was that where Goldberg was clearly a fantasist from the outset, and always destined for a dramatic fall, there was always the feeling that Jordan just might keep things afloat. Even the most sceptical among us begrudgingly started to accept his talk

of a "legacy". Even once we had grown weary of his permatanned posturing, and despite a spate of stories about late payments and dates with the Inland Revenue, we chose not to listen to rumblings from the Cassandras among us. Ignoring for the moment the unfathomable double-speak of Jordan's business dealings - a dodgy lease here, a loan shark there - we can reflect on his achievements in terms that we understand, and conclude that the Jordan dynasty will ultimately go down as one of failure. The decision to dispense with Coppell - although I prefer to think that was down to Steve trusting his own instincts - was only the first of a series of poor managerial decisions, and while he struck lucky with Iain Dowie, the half season that saw Palace clamber from the wrong end of the table to scrape into the Premiership represented one of the few successes in a decade of mediocrity. There were good times, it's true, but too few; we made the headlines with "bouncebackability", and the emergence of Andy Johnson as a striker to compare with some of the best made us feel like a serious club for a while. However, these were interludes in an era bracketed by the managerial mundanity of Trevor Francis and Peter Taylor. Neither can Neil Warnock's tenure be viewed as much more than treading water, and by the end of his time he was transformed from "legend" to "Judas", neither of which remotely apply to the blameless manager.

The minutiae of Jordan's final meltdown will no doubt emerge one day, and perhaps it will make for a good story, as did the complex boardroom shenanigans of Goldberg and Venables, but a few bare facts already seem apparent. The seeds of Jordan's failure were sown when he brokered the deal to wrest control of Selhurst Park from Ron Noades, which at the time he trumpeted as the key to Palace's future stability. It was absurd for him not to have dealt with the issue when he first got involved, and if he really had been bringing the club and the ground together again it would have been laudable, but it later emerged that the new owners of the Freehold were a property company without Ron's emotional attachment to Palace and whose massive rent increases were hidden from the fans. It turned out that Jordan had no more claim to own the ground than I do, and "disingenuous" is the politic way of describing his claims at the time. The suspicion remains that the deal was born of nothing more than a personal dislike or mistrust of Noades - understandable, perhaps - but this was an indicator that Jordan's ego was always likely to cloud his commercial judgement. Whoever owned the ground, the expectation was that at last it would be tarted up a bit, if not completely overhauled, but it remained the shabby, utilitarian mess that it has always been. Each corner of Selhurst Park bears the hallmarks of its age; the old main stand is more or less as it was in the twenties and the years have not been kind to it, and Arthur Wait's jerry-built edifice opposite certainly does the job of making visiting fans unwelcome. A trip to the toilets is not to be recommended, except as a reminder of how little thought is given to the comfort of the paying customer.

This disregard for the very people who pay the wages has been the common theme throughout Jordan's time, and if the dip in attendances was a factor in Palace's financial downfall, then there is a certain poetic justice. Against a background of commercial underachievement and falling crowds, there were also some disastrously expensive player purchases. We should remind ourselves that Ade Akinbiyi had already earned the nickname Akinbadbuy at Leicester, yet Palace apparently shelled out £2.2million, as well as adding hugely to the wage bill. It was a similar story with the plodding Shefki Kuqi, who at least gave us a bit of slapstick, and a couple of flashy drag-backs in the play-offs for Bristol City convinced Warnock that Nick Carle was worth nigh-on £1million. He was wrong.

The fall, when it came, was sudden and shocking, but we can see now that it should have come as no surprise. Stories of late payment of players' wages were treated with an unconcerned shrug by Jordan and his acolytes, and as fans we just accepted the line that temporary cash flow problems would be sorted out soon enough. The chairman's apologists, some despite their better judgement, had convinced themselves of Jordan's business credentials, and the tone of debate on the BBS and Holmesdale internet forums was far from hysterical. I count myself among those who, although a firm critic of the regime, nevertheless assumed that the club was at least solvent, for which I was grateful. Even when the Inland Revenue's winding-up order was revealed, this was presented as commonplace brinkmanship for businesses owing tax, but what we didn't know at the time was that Jordan had taken out a loan with Agilo, a company whose modus operandi is, in their own words, to "invest in distressed companies and special situations. The fund's main activities include trading distressed debt and investing in unique, proprietary deals and event-driven situations." I'm not entirely sure what that means but, by God, the alarm bells should have been ringing out across SE25.

Jordan persisted in trying to paint Agilo as the villains of the piece, and with Michael Portillo on their board, there can be little doubt what kind of operation they are, but the simple fact is that they exist to profit from the misery of troubled companies, and if you invite a venomous snake into your home, don't feign surprise when it bites you. Formal administration was swiftly followed by a mandatory ten-point deduction, and from the fringes of the play-off places, within days Palace faced a struggle against relegation which turned into one of the most epic sagas of the club's 105 years.

The players heard the news as they disembarked at Newcastle airport for a midweek game, and having only suffered three defeats in the twenty games previously, consecutive home defeats to Swansea, Reading and Coventry quickly took the gloss from a fine Cup run - the highlight being Danny Butterfield's unbelievable hat-trick against Wolves - and we realised that this was now a serious business. Moses was withdrawn from the team and sold to Wigan before he could injure himself,

VICTOR MOSES

Warnock jumped ship to Loftus Road, where he could at least be sure of getting his wages paid, and the Administrator, Brendan Guilfoyle, took a punt on bringing in Paul Hart as the new boss for the remainder of the season, with the very straightforward task of keeping Palace from the drop. The real coup, though, was to bring in Dougie Freedman as his sidekick, and this, more than anything else Guilfoyle could have done, showed a real understanding of the importance of keeping the fans loyal.

As everyone had suspected for months, it all came down to the final day of the season, and a straight shoot-out for survival with Sheffield Wednesday at Hillsborough. The Eagles only needed to draw, and the tense drama of that game deserves a chapter of its own, but the joy - and relief - at the final whistle ranks alongside Villa Park in 1990. Anyone who was at the game will have sung some new songs, but the one that embeds itself in the memory, which we will hopefully never need to revive, was simply "Going down? Are we f***, Minus ten, and we're staying up!"

Even as the convoy of coaches headed home, we knew that the nail-biting was far from over, and that there was hardly a queue of investors foolish enough to secure the club's future. There was speculation about the usual suspects getting involved, and even some unusual ones, such as New York rapper P Diddy and Colonel Gaddafi's footballing son Saadi. By all accounts, it really was touch and go as the deadline approached for Palace to exit administration, and we were hours away from having to find a new team to support, or start our own, as AFC Wimbledon had so successfully. The main sticking point was the ownership of the ground, and maybe I'm delusional, but the positive media coverage of the fans' various heartfelt demonstrations helped to force the hand of the bank, who eventually agreed to sell to CPFC 2010, the consortium of true red-and-blue businessmen who not only bought the club and the ground, but earned an enormous stock of goodwill from the fans which they may need to draw on if times get hard.

2010-11

"Just 45 minutes into the season, and we're already top of the table. It looks like they got it right with Burley..."

The new owners, CPFC2010, were a group of four Palace-supporting businessmen: Martin Long, Stephen Browett, Steve Parish, and Jeremy Hosking, who came across immediately as sensible, honest and open, and approached the task of keeping Palace alive almost as if they felt it was their duty to look after the club and listen to the fans, whilst being up front about the economic realities. They had pulled off a stunning feat in purchasing the club, together with the Selhurst Park freehold, and had kept their nerve when it looked as if both Clyne and Ambrose would have to be sold, which appeared certain for a while. Jose Fonte had already gone to Southampton to raise funds as Palace entered administration, and a number of other players had already lined up moves with their contracts having expired. Butterfield, Matt Lawrence and Clint Hill all moved on, together with Derry, but perhaps the most disappointing departure was Johannes Ertl, who had slowly but surely grown into his vital defensive role under Paul Hart, and was starting to grow into the kind of player we had missed since Riihilahti's departure. Despite the mass exodus, for the owners to hang on to Ambrose, as well as Neil Danns, Nathaniel Clyne and Julian Speroni, was a major achievement, but the next job was to appoint a new manager.

There was a case for keeping Paul Hart on, and it seemed slightly harsh to discard him after he had achieved his rescue mission, but when George Burley was chosen it seemed quite an imaginative step. Although Burley had failed as Scotland manager, which surely is inherent in the job description, he had a good record at club level with

Ipswich, Derby and Southampton, and had a reputation for getting his teams to play a passing game. It was a master stroke to keep Dougie Freedman on as his assistant, although I for one favoured giving Dougie the job straight away; in fact I would probably have made him player manager given the chance. It was clear that Burley had no money for big signings, but he went about rebuilding the squad with defenders David Wright and Adam Barrett, and midfielders Andy Dorman and Owen Garvan. With left back Julian Bennett also

OWEN GARVAN

arriving on loan, there were quite a lot of new names to get to grips with in the first game, but the one that made an immediate impact was another product of the academy, Wilfried Zaha. Making his first start, as was Kieran Cadogan, Zaha showed some audacious skills that had the crowd almost gasping, and scored the first goal as Palace breezed to a 3-0 lead at half time. That first 45 minutes was almost the peak of George Burley's career, as Palace just about held on to win 3-2, scrambled past Yeovil in the League Cup, then promptly lost the next four games, only scoring one goal in the process. As the influx of loan players gathered pace, three new strikers in the shape of Jonathan Obika, Pablo Counago, and Everton's James Vaughan made Alan Lee's move to Huddersfield inevitable.

Blackburn midfielder Stuart Marrow also joined, along with big defender Antony Gardner, but out of the blue Palace made a signing guaranteed to make the headlines, that of retired Dutch star Edgar Davids.

Davids had apparently ended his playing days at Ajax a couple of years earlier, but had been one of the superstars of world football for many years in a career that took in both Milan clubs, Juventus, Barcelona and Spurs, as well as 74 caps for the Netherlands. His image was instantly recognisable as he wore goggles to protect his eyes while playing, and he had a reputation not only as a highly skilled creative player, but as a "pit bull" in midfield. The question was whether, at the age of 37, he could get back to the fitness required, even at Championship level. The signing seemed uncharacteristic of the new owners' resolutely unflashy approach, and was redolent of Mark Goldberg's time, but Davids was the biggest name at the club since Lombardo, and the prospect was a tantalising one. He must have seriously wondered what he had been thinking when he found himself playing at left back in a team being beaten 3-0 at Scunthorpe.

Of the new strikers, the best by far was James Vaughan, who scored a superb hat-trick against Portsmouth in his second start, but that game apart, the first three months of the season were mostly disappointing and sometimes rank. The first glimpse the home crowd had of Davids was when his awful back pass contributed to QPR's 2-1 victory, and the last was four weeks later when he was in the side beaten 3-0 at home by Swansea to go bottom of Division One. We were getting that sinking feeling with a vengeance, and losing patience with Burley's persistence with a central midfield of Garvan and Dorman, neither of whom seemed able to get a tackle in or get behind the ball when it mattered. Ambrose could

just about get away with that kind of part-time role, as he could turn a game in an instant, but he was out injured for most of the first three months, and Palace simply couldn't afford the luxury of two passengers - make that three passengers when Counago was on - without a fraction of Ambrose's ability.

November brought a sharp improvement, and Garvan redeemed his reputation with two fabulous strikes against Watford before ruining it again with an idiotic sending-off against Sheffield United for abusing the referee, a game which Palace lost 3-2, but nevertheless showed some long overdue passion. The month ended with a 1-0 victory over Doncaster, notable for being Pablo Counago's one and only decent game in a Palace shirt, and the signs were that George Burley's job was safe for now, but two points from the next five games soon put paid to that idea. To lose one game to Millwall may be regarded as misfortune; to lose both looks like curtains, and so it was that after losing 3-0 at the New Den on New Year's Day, George Burley was sacked after an unremarkable six months in charge. It had been a tall order, for sure, to build a team virtually from scratch, but he didn't seem to be willing to adapt his style to suit the players he had, and never seemed able to make his own luck. The players he had brought in simply weren't right for the job in hand, namely ensuring survival, and although few Palace fans mourned his passing, fewer still bore any malice.

Dougie Freedman was immediately installed as caretaker manager, but Steve Parish made it clear on behalf of the consortium that they weren't going to be rushed into an appointment, and wanted to take a considered look at all the options. In the meantime, Freedman set about the task of reshaping the team ready for the battle ahead, and got off to a fine start when Steffen Iversen made his debut against Preston, and scored the only goal. When Palace made an early FA Cup exit to Coventry the following week, Freedman acknowledged that he was just keeping the seat warm for a new manager, and it was soon announced that the man Parish had settled on was Bournemouth's bright young manager Eddie Howe. After chewing it over, Howe turned down both Palace and Charlton to stay at Bournemouth, only to accept the job at Burnley a few days later, so Steve Parish turned at once to his second choice, and offered the job to Freedman. It seemed written in the stars that this day would eventually come, but Parish had absolute faith in Freedman's ability, as well as his unquestionable commitment, and Freedman himself had no hesitation in taking on a job already fraught with dangers. Steve Kember and Peter Taylor had proved that, however much the fans might have adored you as a player, they would be unforgiving once things weren't going so well as a manager. The task wasn't to slowly develop a team and make steady progress while learning on the job, it was very simply to save Palace once again from relegation to the third tier, which Dougie had famously already done with his goal at Stockport a full ten years earlier.

George Burley had tried in vain to get his team playing the kind of passing football he advocated, but it wasn't only bad luck that militated against that possibility, although he had his fair share. Freedman took a different approach, and identified that the first job was to keep a clean sheet, so he made that his absolute priority. He had the good fortune of Vaughan returning for another loan spell until the end of the season, and Scannell back from several months out with a knee injury, but his focus was on repairing what had been

a highly porous midfield and defence. Gardner returned at centre back in place of Claude Davis, but his smartest move was to shift David Wright from left back to a defensive midfield position, bringing in a proper left back, Dean Moxey, in the transfer window. With a central midfield of Wright and Alex Marrow, Palace ground out three draws, then a 1-0 victory against Middlesbrough, only conceding a single goal along the way. It wasn't very thrilling, but the players suddenly seemed to know what they were meant to be doing, and responded to Freedman with diligence and discipline, even Ambrose putting in a tackle here and there.

DAVID WRIGHT

There had only been one win all season away from home, and Freedman's side didn't improve on that record, but at home Palace were continuing to churn out results and move steadily towards safety. Wright continued his hard work in midfield, quietly breaking down opposition attacks and getting rid of the ball as quickly as possible, and with Marrow injured, Fulham's South African international Kagisho Dikgacoi came on loan to do the same job. Freedman also signed another striker, Jermaine Easter, which gave him additional options up front, and with three extremely hard working forwards in Easter, Vaughan and Iversen, the manager was able to largely do without Pablo

Counago, the Spaniard joining Garvan and Dorman in the wilderness.

The contrast between the results at home and away was startling. Palace had gone an amazing eight home games without conceding a goal after winning a true "six-pointer" against Sheffield United, Ambrose reminding everyone what spectacular goals he could score, and in in the next home game - a 3-3 draw with Reading - he scored the fastest goal of the season inside 40 seconds. Although a single point left Palace still precariously just clear of relegation, it was one of the most entertaining games for a long while, with superb performances from Vaughan and Danns, a lovely goal from Easter, and even a missed penalty by

NEIL DANNS

Ambrose. Despite the huge importance of the two points dropped, it was a measure of what a class act Freedman was as a manager when he said of Ambrose: "no mistake, he will take the next penalty and if he misses the next penalty he will take the next one after that, because he is one of the best strikers of the ball at the club and he scores goals." Sure enough, Ambrose scored his next penalty, and the unbeaten home record had stretched to thirteen games when Scunthorpe came to Selhurst Park for what was looking like the biggest match of the season for both teams. By

now Palace had opened up a six point gap to Scunthorpe, who were third from bottom, but Scunthorpe had recently won 4-1 against Neil Warnock's champions-elect QPR, and on their last visit to Palace had won 4-0, so they were never likely to be a pushover. Palace played inexplicably poorly, and Scunthorpe's 2-1 victory meant that we were in for squeaky bum time, or as Ron Noades once delightfully put it, "bicycle clips time."

It is always so much more exciting to go into the final handful of games with something at stake, and that has been the norm at Palace for the majority of my 43 years as a fan, but this time I felt a little cheated by the quiet, efficient way that the team ground out the points needed for safety. David Wright's return helped them to a point at Doncaster and three against Leeds, and then the final confirmation of safety came way up at Hull. As it turned out, the point won with a late equaliser wasn't needed, but what a way for the unheard of 18-year-old local boy Ibra Sekajja to make his mark with his very first touch of the ball, and what a way to celebrate, with a back flip, that Freedman confessed would have been beyond him. Although the final home game against Forest was rendered meaningless for Palace, and was lost 3-0, the mutual appreciation between the players and the fans during the lap of honour at the end of a tough season was heartfelt, and fully deserved on both sides.

Goalkeepers

In his seven seasons in goal for Palace, **Nigel Martyn** only missed a handful of games, and was a constant presence under Steve Coppell, Alan Smith and Dave Bassett, until he finally left for Leeds, then in the Premiership. When he had first arrived from Bristol Rovers, soon after Liverpool had hit nine goals past Perry Suckling, he already looked top class and he got better and better over the years at Palace, becoming possibly the finest keeper in the country, although a succession of England managers didn't quite realise it, as he only won three caps in his time at Palace. He went on to play for many years at Leeds, then at Everton, proving what a marvellous player he was, becoming a crowd favourite at both clubs, and winning plenty more England caps. By staying at Palace following two relegations from the Premiership he undoubtedly harmed his international career, but the comparisons with the great John Jackson (my first footballing hero in 1968) don't stop there. My one encounter with Martyn sums up for me what a solid, unassuming character he was, happy to chat about a game that Palace had just lost to a stranger standing in front of him in a queue. This wasn't in a West End nightclub, or a swanky dinner dance, but in the Croydon branch of Argos, where I just don't expect to see my footballing heroes.

Martyn was a huge presence in goal, and his calm demeanour gave the defence in front of him great confidence. He didn't look like an acrobat, but had tremendous positional sense and you got the feeling that he studied the art of goalkeeping in great depth, and was always learning. There was nothing flashy, nothing archly eccentric like so many goalkeepers, but he was everything a goalkeeper should be; commanding, agile, and exceptionally strong. He made a few fumbles here and there, and his form dipped along with the team's when goal difference

meant relegation in 1993, but before that he was part of probably Palace's finest defensive line that conceded only 41 goals on the way to finishing third in the pre-Premiership Division One. He did get sent off once, when a rush of blood brought him careering out of the box to poleaxe Wimbledon's Robbie Earle, but that kind of misjudgement was rare indeed. Martyn's sheer strength enabled him to make some memorable point blank saves as well as spectacular dives and penalty saves at full stretch, and because of his positioning and quick reactions, his fingertips were rarely too far from any shot that did beat him. The very last goal he conceded for Palace did leave him stranded, watching helplessly as the ball sailed past him, but Steve Claridge can be blamed for not hitting the ball as well as he should have.

NIGEL MARTYN

With cover so rarely needed for Martyn, **Rhys Wilmot** made only a few appearances, and **Neil Sullivan** and **Bobby Mimms** just one each. After Martyn left, Dave Bassett signed two new keepers and struggled to decide which was his first choice out of **Chris Day** and **Carlo Nash**. Neither was outstanding, but although Nash seemed to have done enough to retain his place in the Premiership, Steve Coppell signed the well-padded **Kevin Miller** from Watford, who had a reputation as the best keeper outside the top division. Miller conceded 71 goals as Palace were relegated in his first season, but overall he wasn't dreadful. When he was good, he was no more than that, but when he was bad, he was indescribably so. His second season ended with Palace in administration, Miller in dispute over the imposition of a pay cut, getting ever plumper, and giving a scandalously bad impersonation of goalkeeping as Palace lost 6-0 at QPR on the final day, for which Palace fans have never forgiven him.

Next up in goal was **Fraser Digby**, a solid jobbing keeper throughout the year-long administration, to be followed by Arsenal's **Stuart Taylor** on loan, before Alan Smith signed Palace's first ever overseas goalkeeper, Latvian **Alex Kolinko**. What is it you want from a goalkeeper? Do you want spectacular or do you want safe? Very occasionally you might get both, but not often, and although Kolinko was capable of the most incredible reaction saves, two in a defeat at Watford among the best I've seen, he was just as likely to flap, fumble or collide with defenders and drop the ball. Kolinko was in and out of the side for a while, alternating with the safer but far less entertaining **Matt Clarke**, and got a black eye from Trevor Francis when he allegedly laughed at Clarke conceding a goal. After Kolinko eventually left under a cloud, and Clarke was forced to retire from football, **Cedric Berthelin** and **Thomas Myhre** took over temporarily, and by the time Iain Dowie's team made it to the play-off final against West Ham, **Nico Vaesen** was doing a fine job on loan from Birmingham.

After so long with a string of unexceptional goalkeepers, Dowie managed to bring two new players ready for the Premiership who would turn out to be among the very best in memory. The Argentinian **Julian Speroni** got the nod ahead of Hungarian **Gabor Kiraly** for the start of the 2004-05 season, but after his gaffe against Everton and the four defeats that followed his confidence was in ruins, and Kiraly became first choice for most of the next three years. Where Speroni lacked in confidence, Kiraly had it in spades, and very soon the fans adored him. Goalkeepers are meant to be loco, and although he milked it, that's just what he was. He was easily recognisable by his baggy grey track suit bottoms, widely known as his lucky pyjamas, but there was more to him than attention seeking. The easiest of shots would prompt Kiraly to spring through the air, grab the ball to his chest and roll over for no reason other than to show off, but beneath it all he was a fine all-round goalkeeper.

Like all the best keepers, Kiraly had his nightmare moments, but as his reputation grew he kept Speroni waiting patiently in the reserves, until he fell out with Peter Taylor and went out on loan to West Ham, then to Aston Villa. Bizarrely, Taylor then tried **Scott Flinders** for two games, during which he conceded seven goals, then brought in **Iain Turner** on loan from Everton, who in turn was injured, meaning that he had no choice but to play Speroni. After just two games and some outstanding saves against Sunderland, Speroni himself was injured, so he had to wait until the very end of the season for Taylor to begrudgingly give him a chance, after which he barely missed a game. Having spent so long in the reserves, Speroni could have been forgiven if he had decided to move on, but he wasted no time in showing what he could do, making it impossible for Taylor to drop him. Kiraly moved to Burnley, and the humble Speroni excelled, winning the admiration of the fans who voted him Player of the Year for three years running. Some of Speroni's saves were breathtaking, and he soon earned a deserved reputation as the best goalkeeper outside the Premiership, so that for Palace to keep hold of him during administration was a major, and very welcome achievement.

This gives me a poser: Julian Speroni or **Nigel Martyn** for my team? Both dedicated, unassuming characters, both loyal to the club and the fans through hard times, and both massive crowd favourites. You know the answer, but it's mighty close between them.

Full Backs

The experienced **John Humphrey** was brought in at right back to replace John Pemberton in 1990, and he played a major part in Palace's improvement from the year before in a wonderful defence alongside Eric Young, Andy Thorn and Richard Shaw. Although already pushing 30 when he arrived from Charlton, Humphrey was as fit as anyone in the squad, had a calm, solid look about him, and impressed straight away. Strong in the tackle, and always keen to get forward, in possession of the ball he was always looking up, trying to find an opportunity to play a long angled pass for Wright and Bright, and a hoof was a rarity for the unfussy Humph. Equally rare were goals, but his second of only two for Palace

JOHN HUMPHREY

was brilliantly thumped in from distance against Wolves, all the more memorable for being scored by Humphrey. He was untouchable at right back until Alan Smith sent him out on loan to Reading for three months in the middle of the 1993-94 promotion season, not long after that Wolves scorcher, but to the fans' delight he returned to play his part in winning the title.

Having made it back to the Premiership, Alan Smith experimented with new signings **Darren Pitcher** and **Darren Patterson** at right back, but neither imposed

themselves and Humphrey ended up playing half the season after all, but it wasn't until his replacement **Marc Edworthy** arrived the following year that Palace had another decent player in the No. 2 shirt. Edworthy developed quickly after joining from Plymouth, and betrayed his origins as a winger with his penchant for beating his man and taking the ball forward through the middle, although he was too often caught out of position. At times he would be used as a sweeper in the absence of Andy Roberts, and this role suited him well, but he didn't always convince defensively. Edworthy played a vital role in Smith's promotion side of 1998, and was one of the better players as he captained the side that went straight back down, but one of Terry Venables' most unpopular decisions was to prefer **Dean Austin** at right back, and Edworthy didn't hang around, moving on to Coventry. Edworthy was the sort of player that one could see staying at a club like Palace for many years, and he was a great loss.

Partly because he replaced the popular Edworthy, and partly because he was nowhere near as good, the crowd didn't take to Dean Austin at all, and he lost his place for a while to **Jamie Smith**, with **Sagi Burton** also getting a few games. A single moment, scoring the winning goal at Norwich, repaired Austin's fractured relationship with the crowd, and he became a fixture for the next few embattled years, earning respect at least, if not adulation, from the grateful fans.

Under Steve Bruce, then Trevor Francis, Jamie Smith was again preferred at right back before the arrival of **Curtis Fleming**, past his prime, but a wholehearted attacking full back, whose Palace career was cut short by injury. Into the side came **Danny Butterfield**, and eight years later he was still there, despite a few interruptions along the way. Butterfield had been billed as a right-sided midfielder when he arrived from Grimsby, but he was at his best in defence, often getting forward in support down the right, and putting in some very good crosses. Over the years he had hit a few spectacular goals, his first from a tight angle against Ipswich being especially glorious, and he was often used in midfield or at centre back, but in Butterfield's final year at Palace Neil Warnock put him into the side for an FA Cup replay against Wolves as a makeshift centre forward. Wolves were in the Premiership, and Palace were in administration, but Butterfield scored not just a perfect hat-trick, but the fastest in Palace's history, scoring with his head, his right, then his left within just six minutes. Ridiculous.

The players who had filled Butterfield's boots in the intervening years included **Emmerson Boyce**, an improving defender from Luton, who was one of Dowie's best players in his year in the Premiership, and **Matt Lawrence**, who came in for constant abuse, but gave his all for the cause, as well as writing an unusually witty and entertaining column in the match day programme. Finally Butterfield had to win his place back from **Nathaniel Clyne**, which he did for a period, before Clyne settled into the first team with the potential to become one of the best full backs ever at the club.

On the left of that stable defence of 1990-91 was **Richard Shaw**, who is hard to pigeonhole, as he played for long periods in midfield, and surprised everyone at how adept he became at centre back later in his career. Although naturally right footed, Shaw always did a good job on the left, despite a spate of own goals, and was certainly better than either of his successors,

the disappointing **Paul Bodin** and **Lee Sinnott**. Erstwhile emergency striker **Chris Coleman** was tried before **Dean Gordon** came into the side from the youth team and eventually established himself as Palace's first specialist left back since Mark Dennis in his brief spell some years earlier. Gordon announced his arrival with an unstoppable goal from a long range free kick against Forest, and later in the season galloped forward to score a stunning late equaliser against Derby, one that confirmed what a powerful weapon Gordon's left foot could be. When asked to step up for a penalty, Gordon took a very short run-up and only had to hit the target, as any goalkeeper foolish enough to get in the way risked life and limb. A good athlete, but totally one-footed, Gordon's strength was in getting forward, overlapping down the left to whip in crosses, or moving onto loose balls outside the area and having a crack. He scored some beauties from distance over the years, and even scored one hat-trick, with two penalties and a header, and when Palace played with a sweeper system he found himself in his element as an attacking wing-back.

When Dean Gordon was injured for a long period, **Jamie Vincent** seemed his natural heir, having looked good in his few appearances and scored a Gordon-like goal with his left foot against Southend, but instead he moved to Bournemouth and Dave Bassett brought Australian left back **Kevin Muscat** into the side. Muscat was not yet notorious as one of football's most appalling thugs, but we saw plenty of that side of him in his time at Palace, where he was also used at right back and in midfield. Once Gordon had eventually gone, the left back position was a problem which wasn't solved by the costly failure of **David Amsalem** or the on-loan **Jason Crowe**, and it was a great pity that Chinese international

Sun Jihai didn't stay longer than one season, as he was improving rapidly.

Jamie Smith was tried at left back for a while, but with no money to spend Steve Coppell did well to get two very good players on loan to plug the gap. The first was the highly reliable Terry Phelan, who was as solid one would expect, and he was followed by an obscure Arsenal youth team player, Ashley Cole. Cole was outstanding from the start, and played a big part in helping Coppell's young side survive the post-Goldberg administration season. For a short while we thought that Palace might be able to keep him, but Cole's performances at Selhurst Park had put him in the reckoning at Highbury, and he was soon way beyond our reach.

Perhaps it is unfair to compare Cole with his successor Craig Harrison, but Harrison didn't pull up any trees before Steve Staunton came on loan for a short while, his most memorable contribution being an extraordinary goal past the stranded Tranmere keeper from nearly the halfway line. Next up at Number 3 was Danny Granville, an improvement on Harrison, but an unremarkable player, although he did have something of a renaissance under Iain Dowie before losing his place to Gary Borrowdale. Granville and Borrowdale alternated for a while until Tony Craig's short spell was ended by the arrival of Clint Hill. Brought in by Warnock to toughen up the team, Hill would have fitted well in Iain Dowie's boxing-fixated side, and mostly stayed just the right side of the line between uncompromising and plain dirty. Mostly.

All the while that Hill was at left back, Lee Hills could never establish himself after progressing from the youth team, but with Hills injured, George Burley started his season with Julian Bennett on loan from Nottingham Forest. David Wright, Matt Parsons and even Edgar Davids all had a turn at left back, before Dougie Freedman signed Dean Moxey from Derby, against whom he scored a stunning left foot goal which got me thinking about the good old days of Deano.

DEAN GORDON

Frankly, there is no real competition for Dean Gordon for the left back position during this era, but right back is more vexing. Clyne could turn out to be the best yet, Edworthy should have stayed longer, and Butterfield deserves recognition for his loyalty and consistency, but for the part he played when Palace qualified for Europe (yes they did) I have to stick with John Humphrey.

Centre Backs

According to reserve keeper Andy Woodman, **Eric Young** was "a cold, blunt bastard, but not a bad bloke." If you can't have a Bobby Moore or Franz Beckenbauer in defence, what you really do want is at least one cold, blunt bastard, and Young gave the team a hard centre that had been lacking with Gary O'Reilly. Young and **Andy Thorn** renewed their partnership from their days at Wimbledon, and for a few years the pairing was as good as any we had seen at Selhurst Park. Wearing a headband to protect his forehead during games, Young became known as "Ninja", and was as fearlessly strong in the tackle as in the air, scoring a few goals as well

ERIC YOUNG

as creating many more whenever he went forward to create havoc from free kicks and corners. Young's style gave ammunition to those who put Palace's success down to their strong-arm tactics, and one might never have guessed that he was a trained accountant. Not averse at times to dishing out the odd elbow, I still never saw Young as essentially a dirty player, more a wholehearted and single-minded stopper, with more skill than many realised, but he met his match when Martin Keown's craven revenge attack put him out of action for five months. Young came back as strong as ever, became a regular in the Wales side, and was at the heart of Alan Smith's promotion-winning team of 1994, alongside fellow Welsh international Chris Coleman. By now we had seen the best of Ninja, and Smith ignored him for most of the following Premiership season, but there is no question that Young was one of the very best central defenders Palace have had.

Andy Thorn was perhaps the junior partner in the pairing with Young, but his contribution to Palace's excellent defence was just as valuable. His forays forward were a key weapon, with several goals coming from his near post flicks from corners, and it was his goal that knocked Liverpool out of the League Cup one famous night in 1992. Thorn was replaced at centre back the following year by **Chris Coleman**, who at last found his niche after being used as a left back, and as an emergency striker for quite a spell. Once he had settled into the centre back role alongside Young, for a while his Wales team mate, Coleman looked a natural and his partnership with **Richard Shaw** the following season was equally effective despite having a very difficult time in the Premiership. While not as powerful as Eric Young in the air, Coleman was confident with the ball and read the game very well, but once Palace were relegated in 1995 he appeared to have become more interested in getting a deal with a Premiership club, eventually joining Blackburn, where he did reasonably well for a season before moving on to Fulham. Shaw himself had spent most of his time at Palace either at full back or in midfield, but despite his lack of height, he had become a very good reader of the game and surprisingly played some of his best football as a centre-back alongside Coleman.

Palace struggled to adequately replace Coleman and Shaw as they headed for the play-offs under Dave Bassett, and although **Andy Roberts** often did a fine job in defence, **Gareth Davies** - yet another Welshman - was in and out of the side, **Tony Gale** and **Jason Cundy** played a few games between them, and **David Tuttle** followed Bassett from Sheffield United to play alongside **Leif Andersen** for a while. Tuttle was passable, and Leif was certainly big, but dreadfully slow and cumbersome, yet between them they helped Palace to the play-offs. Tuttle never really had a decent partner at the back until **Andy Linighan** arrived from Arsenal, and although he was past his very best, the improvement in Palace's defence was considerable. As expected, Linighan struggled somewhat in the Premiership, and while the emergence of Icelander **Hermann Hreidarsson** was promising, the record signing of **Valerian Ismael** at £2.75million was a washout. Ismael had been thrown into a relegation battle in a strange country and with a lot of strangeness going on all around him, and although he showed no signs of being worth the massive fee, he later went on to play at the top level in Germany for double-winning sides Werder Bremen and Bayern Munich. He was never given a chance in the team under Terry Venables, and was sold at a huge loss within nine months of arriving at Palace, leaving us to wonder what might have been.

Two of Venables' best signings, having dumped Ismael and lost Hreidarsson, were the Chinese defender **Fan Zhiyi** and Rangers' Australian **Craig Moore**, although it seems his transfer fee was never paid, and he returned later that season. Moore didn't look or behave like a typical centre back, and was a far better footballer than either Tuttle or Linighan, although a fearless tackler all the same, but a bigger impression was made by Fan, who was equally effective in midfield or at the back. Fan was the captain and star of China's national team, and an issue for the club was always going to be the amount of time he spent with his country, but whenever he pulled on a Palace shirt he gave his all and could never be accused of being a mercenary just going through the motions. He had his rash side, gave away a few penalties and was sent off a couple of times - once for shoving the referee out of the way to get the ball back at QPR - but he played with total commitment and passion. Although only at Palace for three full seasons, there was something about him that chimed with the club and the fans, and it was a sad day indeed when Steve Bruce let him go.

As Palace scraped through administration Coppell gave chances to young centre backs **David Woozley,** and **Richard Harris** who had an almighty long throw and whose last start was in a 7-1 defeat at Huddersfield. Once the club was solvent again, though, it was time to invest in a good centre back, but **Neil Ruddock** wasn't it, starting slowly, and getting slower before his place was filled by a couple of loan players, **Andy Morrison** and **Matthew Upson**, and for the vital last couple of games, American World Cup defender **Gregg Berhalter**.

A regular at centre-back for Australia, **Tony Popovic** was one of Steve Bruce's first signings and although his season was rather fragmented he looked a strong, agile defender, with a natural air of leadership. His best period was possibly when he was paired with **Darren Powell** - Palace's first really big centre back in the classic mould since Eric Young - before losing his place to **Kit Symons**. Although Popovic was generally very popular with the fans, during his five seasons at Palace he wasn't always first choice, but was always ready to step back up from the reserves. He was a little erratic, and his elegantly executed back heel to score an own goal against Portsmouth capped a very difficult introduction to the Premiership under Dowie, who later dropped him for **Gonzalo Sorondo**. By that time, "One Size" **Fitz Hall** was first choice at centre back, and **Mark Hudson** had made a permanent move from Fulham, while there was further competition for places from **Mikele Leigertwood** and the "Peckham Beckham", **Darren Ward**.

Hall was one of the better performers in his first season, and initially formed a solid partnership with Darren Ward the following year, while Leigertwood turned out to be a useful utility player in a number of positions in defence and midfield, a little like Richard Shaw had been. Ward's form fell away, and Peter Taylor's preferred centre backs were Hudson and his own signing **Leon Cort**, renowned for the scarcity of his bookings throughout his career. Cort looked every bit as good as Hall had been, and was possibly Taylor's best purchase, but he wasn't rated by Neil Warnock, and was replaced at the back by **Jose Fonte**. Fonte settled in alongside Hudson, who was succeeded by **Paddy McCarthy**, a very similar player to Hudson, but perhaps a little more aggressive. Although Fonte had a reputation for being able to play the ball out of defence, we didn't see too much evidence, and both he and McCarthy were prone to basic errors at times, often found ball-watching as crosses were whipped in between them. To stiffen the back line, Neil Warnock signed Derby's notoriously brutal **Claude Davis**. In his time at Palace, Davis was at times a rock, throwing himself fearlessly into challenges, but at others was a liability; he could show deft skill to go past players, or he could let them in for a chance on goal with a complete howler. With Fonte being sold to Southampton, Davis got more games than he might have expected, or we might have hoped, but was eventually usurped the following season by the loan signing and proud owner

of one England cap **Anthony Gardner**, unquestionably a more sophisticated player than Davis, and less nerve-wracking to watch.

FAN ZHIYI

I imagine that few who saw **Eric Young** in his pomp would disagree with him being selected for this team, but the other place is difficult. Chris Coleman would have his supporters, as would Tony Popovic and Jose Fonte, maybe even Fitz Hall, but as I'm selecting just my favourites, the other shirt has to go to the unique **Fan Zhiyi**.

Midfielders

The central midfield partnership of **Andy Gray** and **Geoff Thomas** continued to serve Palace well following the FA Cup final defeat, and earned them both England recognition, although Andy Gray's involvement was limited to half a game for his country. They both had possibly their best seasons as Palace confounded everyone by finishing third in 1991, and with the maverick Andy Gray complementing Thomas' outstanding endeavour, the two of them dovetailed beautifully on the pitch. Thomas fully deserved his England place, and was an example to everyone with not just his relentless hard work and athleticism, but his strength in possession, vision when passing to the front men, and ability to arrive late in the box for powerful headed goals. Geoff Thomas was the best all-round midfielder I have ever seen at Palace, but as he made it into my team for the 1969-1990 period, I shall leave him out of my calculations for this volume. Gray had a good range of skills as well as a dangerous long throw and powerful shot, but was very different in character to Thomas and more likely to fly off the handle. He was sent off following a scrap with the similarly undisciplined Dennis Wise in a game against Chelsea which Palace won at Selhurst Park, and was always prone to rash reactions, so Coppell finally had enough of his attitude problem. Feeling that Gray was not pulling his weight in training or in games, the manager put him up for transfer as a wake-up call and Gray sulked off to Spurs, which opened the way for first **Simon Osborn**, then **Gareth Southgate** to make the step up to the first team.

Unlike his fellow "Bisto kid" Simon Rodger, Simon Osborn never really entrenched himself in Steve Coppell's side, ultimately appearing a little lightweight, although he later moved on to have a long and successful career at a number of other clubs, mostly at Championship level. On the other hand, once Gareth Southgate got his hands on the shirt, he kept it. Southgate had come through the youth system and into the first team initially as a right back, filling in for John Humphrey for a spell, but as he developed his best performances for Palace were in midfield, from where he went on to captain his club. His first goal on the opening day of the 1992-93 season against Blackburn was a stunning long range effort, but Blackburn's new signing - and Southgate's future England colleague - Alan Shearer had to go and trump it with two fabulous goals of his own. Although Palace were relegated that year, they bounced straight back under Alan Smith, with Southgate having a superb season as captain, and bursting forward to score more terrific goals, none better than the outstanding solo effort against Portsmouth. Southgate caught the eye during his final season at Palace, and moved on to become an outstanding centre back for Aston Villa and England, but it was in Palace's midfield that he developed into a top class player.

There were a number of bit part players in Palace's midfield during Southgate's time, such as the coltish and nimble **Bobby Bowry**, and **Ricky Newman** who played virtually a full season in the Premiership and scored three goals of quality, but neither really developed and moved on to have good careers at Millwall. **Darren Pitcher** was another utilitarian defensive midfielder who never really sparkled, although he scored a memorable cup goal against Wolves which left the ball satisfyingly lodged in the stanchion. He was guilty of some dreadful brutality in midfield at times, and his replacement **Ray Houghton**, arrived just too late to help Palace avoid the drop in 1995. Houghton was the wise head so desperately needed in Alan Smith's young side and one could see the quality that he brought straight away. Houghton had done it all with Liverpool and latterly Aston Villa, and although he was 33 years old, he had more energy than any of the younger players and put them to shame with his work ethic. The previous summer he had scored a famous goal for Ireland in the World Cup to beat Italy, and for a struggling Premiership side such as Palace he seemed just the man for the job.

DAVID HOPKIN

Houghton had an excellent second season, linking well with the newly arrived Dougie Freedman and another recently acquired Scot, **David Hopkin**. Having never quite made his mark at Chelsea, the signing of Hopkin by Steve Coppell turned out to be one of his very best, and he very quickly became a favourite at Selhurst Park with his wholehearted commitment and no-nonsense approach. Not the prettiest, with his wingnut ears, ginger hair and missing front teeth, all the clichés about Celtic warriors applied to Hopkin and if there was a loose ball to be won, he would make it his no matter who was in the way. He was destructive and creative in equal measure and scored a host of superb goals during his first two seasons, typically lashing the ball home with either foot with apparent disdain. His finest moment came with the last minute winner at Wembley against Sheffield United, by which time he

had become a valuable commodity, and it was the greatest of shames that he moved on to Leeds straight afterwards.

Arriving at Selhurst Park at the same time as Hopkin was **Andy Roberts**, at the time Palace's most expensive purchase, from Millwall. Played sometimes in central defence, sometimes in midfield, Roberts was generally thought of as a sweeper, and during his first season he looked like he could develop into an England player in time. His goal against Leicester in the play-off final was about the first time he had advanced over the half way line all season, as his job was to pick up the ball deep and feed Hopkin and Houghton ahead of him. Often he could hit a sweet long pass up-field, or thread a delicate ground pass through an impossible gap, but after a while he seemed to become all about the style, and started to look slow and a little lazy, despite becoming team captain. He finally fell out of favour after a poor season in the team that included Lombardo, and made a surprise move to Wimbledon as the squad was just about to be dismantled.

By this time **Simon Rodger** had returned to the midfield, with a succession of moderate players like **Carl Veart** and **Jamie Fullarton**, who had no place being in the Premiership, and **Neil Emblen**, the answer to a question nobody asked. Towards the end of that desperate season with Lombardo ostensibly in charge, Mark Goldberg, having failed to entice Paul Gascoigne, spent one of the millions that he never really had on Sasa Curcic, the talented but troublesome misfit from Aston Villa. For a while Curcic had gone missing - not for the first time - apparently to sort out a work permit, but it was telling that his Villa manager John Gregory wasn't too worried: "He had to get some papers but if he has gone home he might have been grabbed to do National

Midfielders

Service. To be honest, I'm not bothered about him." The saga dragged on for some weeks, but once Curcic announced that he had just married a girl that he met in Asda, the problem with the work permit vanished, and he was free to sign. Tales of Curcic's unprofessional behaviour are legion, including how he went AWOL from Villa in order to have a nose job, and he was essentially a party animal with too much money, and too many drugs to spend it on, but - and this remains a guilty pleasure - he was fantastic to watch, even more so when sporting his peculiar bleached goatee. A born crowd-pleaser, it came as no surprise to find out that since retiring Curcic went on to win Serbia's version of Celebrity Big Brother. Perhaps it was his reputation more than what we actually saw, but it seemed senseless at the time that players such as **Nicky Rizzo** and **Craig Foster** were playing while Curcic wasn't even on the bench, although we can now surmise why that was.

As Goldberg's fantasy crumbled, Steve Coppell soldiered on with the midfielders that were left, and Craig Foster deserves some credit, as well as **Steve Thomson**, but at the heart of Coppell's midfield for the most testing of years was Simon Rodger, until **Hayden Mullins** moved forward from central defence to become a highly accomplished player in the middle. Mullins was ready as soon as he made the step up to the first team, and from the start had a calm air that was vital at that nervy time. He was unflustered in possession, a good tackler, and always looking to play the ball to feet. Naturally defensive, and perhaps generally one-paced, he got forward to score ten goals in one season, and his performances never dipped, no matter what position he was asked to play in. He had a touch of class that was maybe wasted in a struggling team, but remained consistently

one of Palace's best players under Steve Bruce and Trevor Francis, waiting patiently for Premiership football again until moving sideways to West Ham. A year later Iain Dowie took Palace up, beating Mullins' new team in the play-off final.

One of Alan Smith's first signings after Simon Jordan's takeover was **Jamie Pollock**, whose portly presence acted as ballast for Palace's slide down the table, and the return of David Hopkin was a disappointment, but Smith made his best acquisition when he signed **Aki Riihilahti**, a Finnish international midfielder, from Norwegian side Valerenga. He came straight into the team and made a key contribution to survival, scoring one of the goals that beat Portsmouth and playing in the last day victory at Stockport, but he really blossomed the following season under Steve

AKI RIIHILAHTI

Bruce. In a match day programme Q&A feature, Dougie Freedman was asked: "If you weren't a footballer, what would you be?" and his answer was "Aki Riihilahti"; Aki himself would be unlikely to take offence, highly aware as he was of his strengths and weaknesses. He was no Sasa Curcic; in fact you could say he was the antithesis of Curcic in every respect bar one, that the crowd loved him. Although categorised as a defensive midfielder whose job it was to break up play - and he was one of the best we've seen at that job - he wasn't the sort of player to hover around the centre circle, but would arrive late in the box to score some vital and memorable goals, inviting comparisons with Geoff Thomas. He was nowhere near as good on the ball as Thomas, but his relationship with the Palace fans bore comparison with that of Thomas, and as I'm selecting my team of the era on the basis of my favourite players, Riihilahti is, as we fantasy managers say, the first name on the team-sheet.

When **Shaun Derry** came into the side under Trevor Francis, the first impression was of a fairly ordinary midfielder, with a range of misguided hairstyles, who would graft away in a team whose ambitions didn't go beyond finishing in the middle of the table, and to me it felt like Derry fitted well with the general atmosphere of mediocrity prevalent while Francis was around. When Steve Kember took over, nothing had changed, and Derry was one of many players who looked so poor during the 5-0 defeat at Wigan that turned out to be Kember's last. Iain Dowie used him less and less, and by the end of the season he was generally on the bench, and not expected to have a role to play in the play-offs. For the final in Cardiff it seemed a most peculiar decision to replace the suspended Julian Gray on the left with Shaun Derry, whose appearances to date had all been deep in central midfield, but Derry's disciplined performance was a revelation, and I saw him in a different light at last. He soon moved on once Palace were promoted, but when Neil Warnock brought him back to the club three years later he immediately made a huge difference to the team, and made me wonder whether I hadn't really been paying attention before. He gave the midfield what it had been missing since Riihilahti, and although he wasn't as mobile

as Aki, his energy and determination in the defensive role made him a natural to captain the team, which he did superbly as Palace recovered from the ten point deduction in 2010. Derry's passing could be patchy, but when he was on song he was more than just a destroyer, and did a lot of good work around the opposition box, although goals weren't his thing.

While Derry had been away, **Michael Hughes** had done a sterling job in the middle before falling out of favour under Peter Taylor, despite still having plenty to offer, and two youngsters had come through to become fixtures in the team. **Ben Watson** and **Tom Soares** really established themselves during Dowie's season in the Premiership, and continued as regulars under both Peter Taylor and Neil Warnock before both leaving for Premiership clubs. Watson, whose best performances earned him the fanciful nickname "the ginger Zidane", had looked something special when we first saw him as a 17-year-old, but he took a while to develop into no more than a solid but inconsistent central midfielder, a good striker of a dead ball, and an excellent passer, but only on his day. He started out looking as if he would become a great player and although at Palace he only ever became very good, perhaps there is still time. Tom Soares was a different type of player; tall, highly athletic, very occasionally willing to take players on and head for goal, but he spent a lot of time out of position as a wide player on the right, and I could never quite work out what he was doing, or why he was so often in the team.

Carl Fletcher was an honest, diligent player who was seen as one of Taylor's men and gradually dropped out of Neil Warnock's plans. **Nick Carle** was a creative midfielder who never really got going at Palace, and

Midfielders

if Warnock thought that Palace were "too nice" when he arrived, that was never going to be an issue with **John Oster**. French youngster **Alassane N'Diaye** was briefly the next big thing, ending up as a squad player, but one of Warnock's early signings, **Neil Danns**, eventually came good after being out injured for most of his first year. An energetic, busy player, who covered a lot of ground in all areas of the pitch, Danns got better and better throughout his difficult final season, and it was a great pity when he left for Leicester.

George Burley's brand new midfield pairing of **Owen Garvan** and **Andy Dorman** had no bite to it, and all we could say of the once-great **Edgar Davids** was that he really should have stayed retired. With the pressing need to erect a dam in midfield, Dougie Freedman turned to another of Burley's men, **David Wright**, who proved the key player as the defence shut up shop for the year, assisted variously by the promising **Alex Marrow**, and the commentator's nightmare, **Kagisho Dikgacoi**, scorer of probably the most accidental goal ever seen at Selhurst Park.

My midfielders for the team of 1990-2011 come down to just a handful, but the players that stand out for me are Derry, which I would never have thought possible after his first spell, Southgate and Mullins, two of Palace's finest ever youth products, and my final two, **David Hopkin** and - no great surprise - **Aki Riihilahti**.

Wingers

When Steve Coppell set about strengthening the side in 1990, one of the areas that he identified as a weakness was wide on the left, and when **Glyn Hodges** arrived from Watford, it looked like the end of the line for **Phil Barber**, who had toiled manfully for the past seven seasons, since the days of Alan Mullery. To play in the FA Cup final was a great achievement for a player with such limited ability as Barber, but endeavour can often be as important, and on that score he was peerless. However, Coppell needed more quality in order to progress in the top flight, and Hodges had a reputation as a skilful player and sometime Welsh international who had followed Dave Bassett from Wimbledon to Watford, and perhaps belonged in the top division. A South London boy, Palace seemed a good fit for him, but he disappointed in his first few appearances, and was regularly substituted, looking patently unfit. He did score one of the eight goals against Southend in the League Cup, but that was just about his only meaningful contribution at Selhurst Park before he was farmed out to rejoin Bassett at Sheffield United before the season's end. In fact the best we saw of Hodges was the following season, when he scored a peach of a goal for United against Palace, and looked decidedly trimmer, but he has to go down as one of Coppell's first misjudgements since promotion to Division One.

Hodges' failure meant a stay of execution for Barber, but in what turned out to be an unusually settled side that finished third in the table, first choices on the wings were **John Salako** and **Eddie McGoldrick**, who provided the ammunition for Wright and Bright in the middle. Salako had come into his own during the previous season's cup run, but this was the year that he really started to shine, and started to score goals as well as create them. The beauty of Salako was that he could not only play comfortably on either wing, but would cross with either foot and this enabled him to keep defenders guessing. It wasn't too often that he would push the ball past the full back and gallop into the space, as his trademark was his close control and ability to change direction and run with the ball. Indeed, his tendency was to cut inside and head down the middle, and for a while he was used more centrally, and was a good finisher, even placing a deft header past Neville Southall in the ZDS final at Wembley. He did a good job in goal once, when Nigel Martyn was sent off against Wimbledon, and the part that

JOHN SALAKO

he played in Palace's best ever season earned him a deserved England call-up. One particularly memorable goal was the long distance lob at Nottingham Forest, but early on in the 1991-92 season he jumped to head a ball goalwards and as he landed his knee was bent backwards, causing what many feared would be an injury to end his career in football. His rehabilitation from surgery was long and arduous, but he came back fighting fit in time for the start of the next season and any fears that he might not be the player he was were soon dispelled, earning him a recall to the England squad, before injury once again put him out of action for another ten months. An articulate and telegenic player, it looked for a while as if his future would lie behind a

Wingers

microphone rather than on the pitch, but with tremendous determination he came back once again, and even scored a hat-trick in his first game back, going on to play a major part in Alan Smith's side that went up to the Premiership as runaway champions. As a key player during several of Palace's best seasons, and as one of the finest players to come through Palace's juniors, he would be a very hard act to follow, and I would select him for my team of the era.

On the other flank in 1990-91 was Eddie McGoldrick, a winger almost by accident. Some, and possibly McGoldrick himself, felt that his best position was as a sweeper, and Steve Coppell used him in that role when he thought the game required it, but having been a key member of the promotion side of 1989, at first his slight frame didn't seem equipped for the rigours of the top division. Although not blessed with Salako's range of skills, McGoldrick's close control made him hard to dispossess when he had his head down, and his final ball was usually accurate and inviting for the strikers. He also hit a scoring patch in 1992, mostly tap-ins and close range headers, and a fluke long range chip against QPR, and eventually earned international recognition with the Republic of Ireland. Always enjoyable to watch and a key player Coppell's team for many years, it was still a surprise when he left following relegation, the surprise not being that he had gone, but that he had gone to Arsenal.

When **Simon Rodger** came into the first team, at around the same time as Simon Osborn, he wasn't really identified as a winger, but it was evident early on that he had a talent for delivering the kind of balls with his left foot that Mark Bright in particular thrived on. That left foot was also a potent weapon at corners, where the near post flick on from Thorn or Young

was still a favoured tactic. Throughout his long Palace career, spanning eleven seasons, "Jolly" Rodger played in a variety of positions in midfield, as well as at left back, but for me his best performances were as a wide man. Wherever he was asked to play, Rodger was totally committed, and whatever one might have thought of his ability, he was one of the most industrious players at the club for many years. He saw countless managers and chairmen come and go, and each time it seemed as if his Palace career was over, he would come back, from a year out through injury or from loan, as strong as ever. He joined Steve Coppell during his brief stint at Manchester City, and after he was released by Trevor Francis, joined up with Coppell again at Brighton, as befits a Sussex lad. If loyalty and dedication were the sole criteria, Simon Rodger would get into my top side without question.

An exciting young winger who made a big impact early in his career was "Ooh Aah" **George Ndah**, who made his full debut at Anfield in the League Cup together with Bobby Bowry, and was used only intermittently during the next five seasons. Skilful and quick, and deceptively strong, Ndah was beset by injuries and became a perennial second string, despite always causing the opposition problems when recalled to the first team. Another wide player who never really became established was **Damien Matthew**, who made a big contribution to the promotion push of 1994, but it was at that time that **Bruce Dyer** signed from Watford with a big reputation. Another player hard to pigeonhole, Bruce Dyer started out as a winger, but as he developed was used more and more as a striker, becoming a favourite of Dave Bassett down the middle. Dyer seemed to have all the attributes required, namely great strength and speed, but although he did have a couple of seasons where he scored plenty, for me he was never a natural striker and was better used wide on the right. If he had sight of goal, it was anyone's guess whether he would connect with the ball, and if he did, where it might end up.

ATTILIO LOMBARDO

When **Attilio Lombardo** arrived at Palace, it was a very exciting day indeed, and although it is now hard to disassociate that happy day with the implications of Mark Goldberg's involvement, at the time it felt like Palace were about to become a proper Premiership side at last. A seasoned international, and still winning trophies with Juventus, the bald-headed Lombardo was easily recognisable, and easily the most famous player Palace had ever signed. I was so thrilled that I named my shiny, Italian scooter Lombardo in his honour. Although known as a winger, Lombardo spent much of his time at Palace more centrally, although in fact he was all over the place. He had a curious upright running style, but his footwork was so delicate and his passing and movement so subtle that he stood out a mile from a team that included Tuttle, Muscat and Fullarton. What we saw of Lombardo in the Premiership was exquisite, but he missed half the season through injury, and by the time he returned in March, Palace were already doomed. Bizarrely put in charge of team affairs

rather than being asked to play Palace out of trouble, Lombardo was still loved by the fans despite the inevitable relegation. It was amazing that he stayed, and he started the next season well under Terry Venables, but Goldberg's financial collapse meant the end of his surreal and brief stay at Palace.

Among the plethora of new faces bought by Terry Venables - and there may have been other wingers in that cohort who never got a game - was the Australian **Nicky Rizzo**, memorable for scoring one terrific goal against Norwich but little else, and it was to be another couple of years before Palace signed any wingers worthy of the name. **Andrejs Rubins** was a compatriot of Kolinko from Latvia, who had a good run in the team after scoring a priceless long range goal against Leicester in the League Cup, and although he scored a similar goal against Liverpool in the semi-final, he never appeared robust enough for Division One, and melted away. **Tommy Black** and **Julian Gray** were both young Arsenal players who hadn't quite made it, but both looked very good prospects at Palace's level. Initially it was Tommy Black who made the most impact on the right wing, but he gradually went backwards while Gray flourished. Steve Bruce used Julian Gray as an attacking wing-back for a while, but it was as a straightforward winger wide on the left that he became most effective, and had his own moment of glory against Liverpool, scoring a sweet volley and forcing an own goal to knock them out of the FA Cup in 2003. Gray had all the skill and speed required to play on the wing, and had a fair eye for goal, but he too often went missing in games. Sadly, the abiding image of a player who had some outstanding games for Palace is of someone sulkily thinking to himself "I'm better than this lot."

Wingers

As Black and Gray's stars waned, **Wayne Routledge's** was in the ascendency. Having first broken into the team aged 16, it took him a couple of years to establish himself, but he played every single game under Iain Dowie, as the new manager dragged Palace up to the Premiership and swiftly down again, at which point Routledge was off. As a youngster Routledge was expected to have a future as bright as the other Wayne, his contemporary Rooney, and he was certainly talented with good close control and all sorts of tricks, but at times he seemed to have caught a bit of Julian Gray's attitude, so that when he signed for Spurs, before he had developed as far as he might have with Palace, it wasn't quite with everyone's very best wishes.

Fresh from winning Euro 2004 with Greece, **Vasilis Lakis** toiled for a while on the left, as did Germany's **Marco Reich**, but it was Routledge's replacement, **Jobi McAnuff**, who ensured that the loss of young Wayne wasn't felt too keenly. Far more direct than Routledge, and genuinely two-footed, McAnuff could comfortably switch wings or play down the middle and was the architect of many goals for Johnson and Morrison, as well as scoring some important ones of his own such as a winner at Brighton. At times brilliant, at others invisible, McAnuff was ultimately frustrating, as his ability was evident, but I never understood why he became persona non grata at Selhurst Park after he left. An eye-catching player in the Championship, but never making it at a higher level, in many ways his profile matched Palace's but he chose to pursue his dream of Premiership football at Watford, which didn't quite work out. McAnuff was a model of consistency however, compared to **Paul Ifill**, who, when he wasn't laid up with a bad back, seemed in his own little bubble on the pitch. He scored a few enjoyable goals, but was always just about to come back to his best, which never really happened. Nor did we see any of the talent that **Mark Kennedy** had once possessed, after Peter Taylor had brought him to Palace with high hopes, and once Neil Warnock arrived and demanded a bit of grit, he was on his way, along with another of Taylor's failures, **Stuart Green**. Green had scored one superb free kick against Leicester, but was too much of a lightweight to figure in any team put out by Warnock, who experimented for a while with first **Frank Songo'o**, then both **Victor Moses** and **Sean Scannell** on the wing, as well as giving chances to **Kieran Djilali** and **Kieron Cadogan**.

Chelsea's **Scott Sinclair** also came in on loan and featured in the play-offs against Bristol City, and would have been a superb signing if Palace could have afforded him. Instead, both Moses and Scannell, academy graduates with big reputations, were thrown in at the deep end, and both started to develop very quickly in positions that perhaps wouldn't be their first choice. There had always been a lot of buzz about Moses, who was just starting to really dazzle when he was sold to Wigan, but less had been expected of Scannell, and it was gratifying to see how he developed and strengthened over the next couple of years although his future may be as a striker rather than on the wing.

At the start of Neil Warnock's final season, he made possibly his best signing for Palace when rescuing **Darren Ambrose** from obscurity at Charlton. It would be reasonable to dispute the description of Ambrose as a winger, as it would be with Lombardo, but he did play the majority of his games under Warnock in a wide midfield role at least, often switching from right to left during the course of a game. Not on the face of it an archetypal

Warnock player such as Shaun Derry or Clint Hill, Ambrose nevertheless had an outstanding first season, scoring 20 goals in all competitions. His goals weren't confined to spectacular long-range shots, as he got his share of tap-ins as well, but those were the ones that stick in the memory, especially the stunning free kick in an FA Cup tie against Aston Villa from an impossible distance. Nobody in the Palace squad could hit a ball as sweetly as Ambrose, be it a shot on goal or a long pass, although he could also have spells when his corners failed to clear the first defender. His form fell away slightly once Palace were faced with a scrap to recover from the ten point deduction, but despite it looking certain that he would follow Warnock to QPR, he played every game under Paul Hart, and it was fitting that he should score the vital second goal against Sheffield Wednesday to save Palace from relegation. In his second season, under George Burley, Ambrose never looked fully fit and missed a lot of games, but just when you started to wonder whether he was actually on the pitch, he would pop up with another superb goal, such as the spectacular - and crucial - volley in the six-pointer against Sheffield United.

The most recent academy graduate to make his mark in the first team is **Wilfried Zaha**, who scored in George Burley's first game in charge as Palace raced to a 3-0 lead at half time against Leicester. Although that was his only goal of the season, Zaha's audacious skills when played in a wide position throughout the season gave the fans some real excitement in a season that became another rather dour battle for survival, and he may just turn out to be one of the Palace academy's finest, providing he stays intact as his soaring reputation makes him a target for some corrective treatment by defenders - if they can get near him.

Although true wingers have been few and far between during this period, and some have looked good in bursts before drifting off somewhere - Rubins, McAnuff and Ifill spring to mind - my short list really comes down to **John Salako** for his huge contribution over so many years, and **Attilio Lombardo,** for the excitement of seeing him in Palace colours for too short a time, with Simon Rodger and Darren Ambrose next in line.

Strikers

Anyone who succeeded **Ian Wright** and **Mark Bright** up front at Palace was bound to suffer by comparison, as the pair continued their wonderful partnership in the 1990-91 season, and Palace's surprise emergence as title contenders meant that their talent was being more widely acknowledged. This was their fifth season together at Selhurst Park, and both were at the peak of their powers and as thrilling as ever to watch. Where Wright had explosive speed, agility, and eye-catching ball skills, Bright's all round ability was always slightly underestimated, but each benefited from the other's presence, and in their own way they were both able to score any type of goal. Long range shots, scrambled tap-ins, headers from all angles, all were within their compass, but it was Wright who could make a goal from nothing, turn a player and be in on goal in a flash, or see half a chance from distance and subtly lob the keeper as he did on the way to a memorable hat-trick against Wimbledon. Supplied all season by Salako and McGoldrick on the wings, the fans were treated to the best entertainment ever witnessed at Palace, although much of the press couldn't see beyond Coppell's supposed route one tactics. That was one source of goals, certainly, but there was a great deal more to Palace that year, and it was a bitter blow when Wright and Bright were robbed of the chance of competing in Europe.

Once Ian Wright had decamped to Arsenal the following season, Mark Bright went on to prove that he was an outstanding striker in his own right, and was ever present in all competitions, scoring 22 goals. The problem of how to replace Wright, though, was one that took a while to solve, and with **Garry Thompson** having left, and problem child **Stan Collymore** proving a misfit, the squad was very short of forwards. Steve Coppell paid big money for **Marco Gabbiadini**, but it soon became clear that this was one of his poorer decisions. Gabbiadini was a stocky player who never really looked like making it at the top level however busy he was, and despite a handful of decent goals. His best performance came during Palace's 2-1 victory away to Liverpool where he darted in to score with a neat touch at the near post, and he looked best with the ball at his feet, which really didn't suit Palace's pattern at the time. He was by no means dreadful, but Coppell quickly realised his mistake and offloaded him at a loss less than three months after he signed, an embarrassing admission of failure, but the right decision all the same. Young **David Whyte** showed some promise and a good deal of enthusiasm during a spell alongside Bright, but the season ended with defender **Chris Coleman** up front. He actually proved to be a better partner for Bright than his immediate predecessors, but Palace didn't sign another proper striker until Bright himself was about to end his Palace days, moving on to Sheffield Wednesday, with **Paul Williams** coming in part-exchange.

The youngster signed from Millwall, **Chris Armstrong**, played two games alongside Bright without either of them scoring, but for his first appearance at Selhurst Park Armstrong was paired with Williams and straight away looked a real find, walloping a goal from close range, scoring a second with a header, and showing the kind of speed that had been missing since Wright's departure. Even better, he scored another brace the following week at Everton, and could have scored even more in an outstanding performance. Armstrong had a good first season, but still Palace were deficient up front since Salako, who was looking like a possible solution in the centre, was badly injured. Paul Williams, despite good technical skills and a touch of elegance, wasn't robust enough, so Chris Coleman was again used sporadically in the front line as Palace slipped agonisingly out of the Premiership on goal difference. The following season was Armstrong's best, scoring 25 goals in all as Palace won the Division One title, forming a good partnership with Paul Williams and latterly Paul Stewart, and he netted his first hat-trick in the 5-1 demolition of Portsmouth, the best being a memorable flying header. The archetypal Armstrong goal, though, would see him cutting in from deep on the right with his long-striding upright gait, latching on to a through ball, outmuscling and outpacing the defender before hitting a daisy cutter or a rising shot inside the near post.

As Palace looked to make sure of promotion in 1994, it was clear that more power was needed up front, and Paul Williams made way for the on-loan **Paul Stewart**. Stewart made a real impact despite a horrific mullet and only three goals, and it would have been ideal to have kept him in the Premiership, but once again the problem of finding a strike partner for Armstrong who could operate at the highest level wasn't addressed soon enough. The hard working **Andy Preece** was never going to be the answer, although he started brightly enough, and by the time **Iain Dowie** arrived in January the rot had set in. Dowie was just the job, scoring a few vital goals in the league as well as memorable strikes against Wolves and Manchester United in the FA Cup. The goal against Wolves summed up Dowie as he parried the ball with his face before volleying on the turn, and he even had a good chance against United to put Palace into the Cup final, but ultimately he had arrived too late to save Palace's season.

Following relegation, Armstrong left for Spurs, and after a few games Dowie was also

on his way, so Palace began the following season with **Bruce Dyer** as a striker before a brand new pairing of **Dougie Freedman** and **Gareth Taylor** tried their luck. It was Freedman who was an instant success, scoring 20 goals that year, but Taylor's experience was not unlike that of Gabbiadini before him. His failure to score a home goal and the impatience of the crowd led to him being dropped and then sold before the season's end. New manager Dave Bassett tried George Ndah as Freedman's partner for a while before settling on Bruce Dyer again, and with

DOUGIE FREEDMAN

big **Jeroen Boere** offering little, it was Freedman who was left to score the goals that saw Palace into the play-offs. Freedman was completely unlike any of Palace's best recent strikers - Wright, Bright, Armstrong or Dowie - being slightly built and lacking killer pace, but he perhaps had more real skill on the ball than any of them, and his goals were generally elegant, graceful and most of all subtle. Freedman liked to get the ball at his feet and tease the defender rather than push it forward and go hell for leather, as he had exceptional close control and it was impossible to read which way he would take the ball. Once he had worked himself into position, he had the widest repertoire of efficient finishes, using the toe-poke, volley, side-foot, and most pleasingly the delicate lob. Quite apart from his finishing, though, Freedman's positional awareness was second to none, and you could almost see how much he was thinking ahead. It was a great pity that Freedman was never paired with Iain Dowie, but he did form a good partnership with **Neil Shipperley** before losing his place under Steve Coppell and making a surprise move to Wolves.

Dave Bassett's signing of Neil Shipperley gave the forward line a real focus, and both Dyer and Freedman benefitted greatly from his presence as a big target man, although he was no slouch on the ground either, becoming Palace's best centre-forward of his type since Mark Bright. Shipperley and Dyer became Steve Coppell's favoured partnership as Palace progressed through the play-offs, which left Freedman on the bench more often than not, but back in the Premiership, Shipperley himself was replaced by **Paul Warhurst**, one of that season's many costly failures. Warhurst had somehow gained a reputation as a striker since converting from defence some years earlier, and had even been called into the England squad, but on the whole he looked very ordinary at Palace, and he eventually dropped into defence then out of the picture entirely once Venables had taken over. Juventus reserve player **Michele Padovano** cost Goldberg £1.7million for a solitary goal, and **Tomas Brolin**, although playing deeper than expected, failed to score at all, but by the end of the season Shipperley was at last supported by a striker of real quality in **Matt Jansen**.

Following a delicious goal against Villa, Jansen very quickly became a target for a number of clubs, and ultimately spent less than a season at Palace, but in that short time he caught the eye with his control, his speed and his finishing, as well as his

attitude against a background of upheaval and financial uncertainty. He was a similar player to Freedman in many ways, but had a more showy style and scored some lovely goals before inevitably being sold to Blackburn, a great talent lost to Palace. Another young striker who showed glimpses of real promise was **Marcus Bent**, who was developing into a fine player before Venables came along, but one player who did make it was **Clinton Morrison**, who appeared as a substitute at the very end of the season and tapped home a late winner from a cross by Lombardo, not a bad way to start your career.

Although Dyer and Shipperley were initially preferred by Venables, Morrison came in to the side after a couple of months and developed over the season into the player that Dyer should have been. He had good body strength to hold off defenders, a great ability to get into telling positions in the box, and the asset that Dyer lacked, an eye for goal. Although Morrison's place was under threat from new signings **Matt Svensson** and the wooden **Lee Bradbury**, it was him that the fans loved, and he appeared to love them back. Morrison was soon first choice up front, and had a succession of partners who never quite stuck, including **Andrew Martin** and willing **Leon Mackenzie**, but the best was **Mikael Forssell**, on loan from Chelsea. One could see why Forssell was so highly rated, but also why he wasn't quite ready for Chelsea's first team, as he often seemed to need just a little too much time on the ball, or wanted to get everything in place before shooting, unlike Morrison who was all about instinct.

Morrison and Forssell continued together under Alan Smith, but finally **Dougie Freedman** came back to help rescue Palace at Stockport, and the following season formed an astonishing partnership with Morrison. As Palace went top of Division One under Steve Bruce, Freedman and Morrison were in the best form of their careers, and bringing out the best in each other, but Trevor Francis felt the need for more muscle up front, and that was about all he got with **Ade Akinbiyi**. With Akinbiyi injured and out of contention, the next forward to usurp Freedman's place was **Dele Adebola**, who was poor at Palace although he went on to do a good job elsewhere, but by now Morrison had swapped places with Birmingham's **Andy Johnson**, and it looked at first as though we had been landed with fairly ordinary squad player.

ANDY JOHNSON

After a stuttering start, Johnson's Palace career went from strength to strength after the hat-trick against Brighton, and if Freedman was the most skilful player at the club, which he was, then Johnson was the most hard-working and honest, despite a completely unfounded reputation for diving to win penalties. If I was forced to choose between Dougie and AJ for my team of the era, leaving out Ian Wright who was selected in the previous volume, then I would find it impossible to split them. Hence, they both make the team, ahead of Chris Armstrong.

When a portly Neil Shipperley returned to Palace in 2003, he surprised everyone by having a fine season and scoring the play-off winner against West Ham, but back in the Premiership Iain Dowie decided to bring in a number of strikers to support Johnson, and they all flopped, leaving Johnson to plough a lone furrow up front. **Sandor Torghelle** was no better than Bradbury had been, **Nicola Ventola** spent all season on the treatment table, **Ivan Kaviedes** was a complete misfit, and **Wayne Andrews** was a long way from being up to Premiership standard, spending most of his time warming the bench. Back in the Championship, **Jon Macken's** unimpressive form heralded the return of Clinton Morrison, who was once again reunited with Freedman and, for the first time, Andy Johnson. That combination really should have stormed the division, but Palace didn't quite make it, which meant AJ moving onwards and upwards with Everton as Palace stagnated under Peter Taylor.

The fact that Peter Taylor's preferred strike force tended to be **Jamie Scowcroft** and **Shefki Kuqi** ahead of Freedman and Morrison sums up his time in charge, and their successor as the target man, **Alan Lee**, wasn't really any great improvement, although he did come to be appreciated more once he was leaving. It wasn't until **Craig Beattie** joined on loan under Neil Warnock that Palace had another centre forward to get excited about, but his time was all too short, as was that of the less robust but promising **Anthony Stokes**.

When Simon Jordan's house of cards finally collapsed in 2010, Palace were left with very thin resources up front indeed, and ten points deducted. **Freddie Sears'** loan had ended, with his only goal not even counting, **Stern John** was on the injury list after just one game, and **Victor Moses**

Strikers

had been sold, although Neil Warnock had rarely used him down the middle in any case. That left Alan Lee struggling with **Calvin Andrew** and **Sean Scannell**, who was himself not fully fit. Andrew was an asset to have available from the bench, as he would come on and chase every loose ball, jump for everything in the air, and generally charge around, but he never looked like scoring goals. Nevertheless all three, together with Stern John returning at last, played a valuable part in the scrap for survival under Paul Hart, and Lee in particular deserves credit for his effort, and even the odd goal.

George Burley's signing of **Pablo Counago** didn't bear fruit, but he did well to entice the committed **James Vaughan** on loan from Everton and the veteran Norwegian **Steffen Iversen**, who together with **Jermaine Easter** did a solid job once Dougie Freedman took over, but none would make my shortlist of centre-forwards, which comes down to just six realistic candidates over the period covered by this volume. Of course Ian Wright and Mark Bright are there but, like Geoff Thomas, Wright was in my "all-time" team in 1990. Chris Armstrong in particular, and Clinton Morrison were also favourites of mine, but it is without too much agonising that I plump for **Dougie Freedman** and **Andy Johnson,** two very different players who gave so much to Palace - and I don't just mean the goals - over the years.

Postscript (2011)

The more things change, the more they stay the same. Last week I got a letter from the Football Pools, and as I started to open it I could see that it was a cheque. Does anyone else still do the Pools? For years when I was growing up, the man would come to the door every week to collect the coupon (always 8 from 10) and the money, and at home we would check the scores every Saturday as they were read out on the radio, or I would be sent down the road to get the Evening News results edition and an ounce of Old Holborn. Nowadays I can get results, match reports, statistics, pictures and any amount of opinion in a moment, and I don't even put those mysterious crosses in the boxes or check the score draws any more, putting my trust in the infallibility of the computer.

Yet despite the technology, despite the obscene amounts of money in the game, despite the widening gap between the big clubs and the grass roots, what lies at the heart of supporting a club like Palace hasn't changed a bit. I still look forward to every game just as much and need to know every result, every place moved up or down in the table, every tactical formation. I still get that buzz of anticipation that I might witness dazzling forward play or miraculous goalkeeping: once it was Vince Hilaire or John Jackson, now it is Wilfried Zaha or Julian Speroni. Whoever it is a year from now, or 21 years from now, as long as they are in Palace colours they will be doing it for us, the devoted fans.

What would be my "all-time" fantasy team from my first full season as a Palace fan in 1969 up until 2011? Everyone will have their own version, but here's mine. You may dispute whether they are the best, but they are the players I have most enjoyed over the years.

John Jackson
John Humphrey
Kenny Sansom
Eric Young
Ian Evans
Geoff Thomas
Steve Kember
Attilio Lombardo
Don Rogers
Dougie Freedman
Ian Wright

At the moment the club appears to be in good hands, but I still dream of owning Crystal Palace, changing the colours back to claret and light blue and the nickname back to "The Glaziers". Not yet though; the cheque from the Pools was only for £17.95, but there's always next Saturday...

Chris Winter
November 2011
South East London

CHRIS WINTER